Cuban Communism

*Trans-***action** Books

TA-1 Campus Power Struggle/*Howard S. Becker*

TA-2 Cuban Communism/*Irving Louis Horowitz*

TA-3 The Changing South/*Raymond W. Mack*

TA-4 Where Medicine Fails/*Anselm L. Strauss*

TA-5 The Sexual Scene/*John H. Gagnon, William Simon*

TA-6 Black Experience:
Soul/*Lee Rainwater*

TA-7 Black Experience:
The Transformation of Activism/*August Meier*

TA-8 Law and Order:
Modern Criminals/*James F. Short, Jr.*

TA-9 Law and Order:
The Scales of Justice/*Abraham S. Blumberg*

TA-10 Social Science and National Policy/*Fred R. Harris*

TA-11 Peace and the War Industry/ *Kenneth E. Boulding*

TA-12 America and the Asian Revolutions/*Robert Jay Lifton*

Cuban Communism

Edited by
IRVING LOUIS HOROWITZ

Trans-action Books

Published and distributed by
Aldine Publishing Company

The essays in this book originally appeared
in *Trans-*action Magazine

TA Book-2
Library of Congress Catalog Number: 71-96125

Contents

Preface   vii

Introduction   1
Irving Louis Horowitz

Cuban Communism ✓   3
Irving Louis Horowitz

Revolution—For Internal Consumption Only   37
Richard R. Fagen

Student Power in Action   53
Arlie Hochschild

The Revolutionary Offensive   73
Carmelo Mesa-Lago

The Moral Economy of a Revolutionary Society   95
Joseph A. Kahl

Cuba—Revolution Without a Blueprint   117
Maurice Zeitlin

United States-Cuba Relations: Beyond the Quarantine   131
Irving Louis Horowitz

Preface

However diverse their attitudes and interpretations may sometimes be, social scientists are now entering a period of shared realization that the United States—both at home and abroad—has entered a crucial period of transition. Indeed, the much burdened word "crisis" has now become a commonplace among black militants, Wall Street lawyers, housewives, and even professional politicians.

For the past six years, *Trans*-action magazine has dedicated itself to the task of reporting the strains and conflicts within the American system. But the magazine has done more than this. It has pioneered in social programs for changing the society, offered the kind of analysis that has permanently restructured the terms of the "dialogue" between peoples and publics, and offered the sort of prognosis that makes for real alterations in social and political policies directly affecting our lives.

The work done in the pages of *Trans*-action has crossed

disciplinary boundaries. This represents much more than simple cross-disciplinary "team efforts." It embodies rather a recognition that the social world cannot be easily carved into neat academic disciplines. That, indeed, the study of the experience of blacks in American ghettos, or the manifold uses and abuses of agencies of law enforcement, or the sorts of overseas policies that lead to the celebration of some dictatorships and the condemnation of others, can best be examined from many viewpoints and from the vantage points of many disciplines.

This series of books clearly demonstrates the superiority of starting with real world problems and searching out practical solutions, over the zealous guardianship of professional boundaries. Indeed, it is precisely this approach that has elicited enthusiastic support from leading American social scientists for this new and dynamic series of books.

The demands upon scholarship and scientific judgment are particularly stringent, for no one has been untouched by the current situation. Each essay republished in these volumes bears the imprint of the author's attempt to communicate his own experience of the crisis. Yet, despite the sense of urgency these papers exhibit, the editors feel that many have withstood the test of time, and match in durable interest the best of available social science literature. This collection of *Trans*-action articles, then, attempts to address itself to immediate issues without violating the basic insights derived from the classical literature in the various fields of social science.

The subject matter of these books concerns social changes that have aroused the long-standing needs and present-day anxieties of us all. These changes are in organizational life styles, concepts of human ability and intelligence, changing patterns of norms and morals, the relationship of social conditions to physical and biological environments, and in the status of social science with national policy making.

This has been a decade of dissident minorities, massive shifts in norms of social conduct, population explosions and urban expansions, and vast realignments between nations of the world. The social scientists involved as editors and authors of this *Trans*-action series have gone beyond observation of these critical areas, and have entered into the vital and difficult tasks of explanation and interpretation. They have defined issues in a way making solutions possible. They have provided answers as well as asked the right questions. Thus, this series should be conceived as the first collection dedicated not to the highlighting of social problems alone, but to establishing guidelines for social solutions based on the social sciences.

THE EDITORS
Trans-action

Introduction

IRVING LOUIS HOROWITZ

A decade is a good time for taking stock of nations and of men. The Cuban revolution, led by Fidel Castro and by the memory of Ernesto Guevara, has survived this anniversary. For the occasion, *Trans*-action has gathered together a group of scholars intimate with Cuba and knowledgeable of Inter-American affairs generally. What emerges from this collective portrait, if it contains relatively few surprises, does reveal deep and abiding differences in opinion. But perhaps the most surprising item underlying the diversity of opinions and interpretations is the agreement on the facts of modern Cuba.

Cuba is a stable country. There is little to suggest an imminent collapse of the Castro regime. Yet, the basis of Cuban political power remains highly charismatic, and under the control of the generation which made the revolution. Cuba is also a country of economic austerity, compounded by a series of drastic early economic choices that did not work out well (such as mindless industrialization at the expense of agriculture); yet it exhibits the potency of the heroic economy in which "conscience" plays a leading role in the formation and expansion of the national economy. Cuba is also a country which has an explicit internationalist ideology, but manages to exhibit all manner of national parochialisms.

In short, the authors, each in their own way, show that Cuba may be a paradox, but it is not a mystery. Its present levels, no less than its past mistakes and future ambitions, are available for inspection for those who care to look. And if the picture which emerges is sobering, it should not prove disquieting to those seeking détente if not rapprochement between the nations of the western hemisphere. What the authors of these articles succeed in demonstrating is that the "right of each nation to self-determination" may be rhetoric to many nations of the western world—both those who promulgate and those who supposedly benefit from this doctrine. But in Cuba self-determination is a reality. Whatever Cuba does, for better or for worse, for richer or for poorer, its destiny, unlike its history, cannot be parceled out to others. These papers show how that fate will affect all peoples of the western hemisphere and elsewhere.

Rutgers University   *Irving Louis Horowitz*
New Brunswick, New Jersey

Cuban Communism

IRVING LOUIS HOROWITZ

Cuba today is restless and righteous. Her restlessness derives from a universal heating up of the Cold War, over which she has seemingly little control; while her righteousness stems from a feeling that she has made the first socialist revolution in the Western Hemisphere and the model revolution for Third World countries to emulate. The idea of Cuba's being absent from current news, of her disappearance behind a wall of legality erected by the Organization of American States, is not indicative of the dynamics within Cuban society.

On July 26 of this year, the Organization of Latin American Solidarity (O.L.A.S.) convened in Havana. For Fidel Castro and his partisans, not merely in Latin America but throughout the world, July 26 is the founding day of the Cuban Revolution. This paramount anniversary commemorates Castro's assault on the Moncada Barracks in 1953. Despite his speedy capture and imprisonment then, he has continued to celebrate this first strike against the dictatorship of Fulgencio Batista. Castro came to power as leader of the 26th of July Movement, and every year since, the country has turned out for parades and

3

speeches and has had a day off from work on July 26.

In his speech welcoming the O.L.A.S. delegates, Castro momentously echoed Karl Marx: "A specter is haunting the continent. It is the specter of the Organization of Latin American Solidarity, and this specter is causing insomnia among the reactionaries, imperialists, henchmen, *gorilas* [militarists], and exploiters." In fact, however, the Fidelista specter seems to be haunting the communists of the Western world. For Castro's remarks promptly elicited a stinging response from a leading Chilean communist, Luis Corvalán, a response that appeared in *Pravda,* the leading newspaper of the Soviet Communist Party. Corvalán warned: "Any effort by communists to impose their views on other ranks of the anti-imperialist forces does not help the achievement of unity." He added, "Lenin warned against the danger of adventurism, which as a rule results in the loss of precious lives of revolutionaries and the retreat of the movement." What is more, the roster of those absent from the O.L.A.S. meeting is striking. Along with Corvalán, other old-guard Chilean communists boycotted the convention, as did veteran party leaders from Venezuela and Argentina. Even some old Cuban party-liners were conspicuously absent. Despite the meeting's name, then, solidarity was *not* its leitmotiv.

Less than a decade ago, Fidel Castro was the idol of Latin America's communist leaders. Why has he now become a focus of intra-party factional divisions? An even more urgent question deals with Cuban policy, which—like the Chinese—remained relatively prudent from 1962 to 1966. Just what has led to this immense tactical shift toward belligerency? Clearly, these two questions are related, for it is Cuba's shift toward belligerency that has, in large part, estranged her from other communist parties in other countries.

Some of the answers to both questions are suggested in the works of Régis Debray and those imputed to Che Guevara. Debray, a 26-year-old philosophy professor and authority on guerrilla warfare, was absent from the O.L.A.S. meeting, having been detained by the Bolivian military on a charge of practicing guerrilla warfare. Despite his arrest, U.S. readers learned from reviews in *The New York Times* (July 26) and elsewhere that Debray's analysis of the Cuban process, *Revolution in the Revolution?,* is now available in English. Guevara was also away from the meeting, and the officially, and unofficially, encouraged explanation was that Che was off spreading the revolution on other stages—although it should be noted that the style of Guevara's recent pamphlets is noticeably lacking in either the sophistication or humanism that characterized his earlier writings. At the conference, the O.L.A.S. delegates named him Honorary President *in absentia.*

The writings of Debray and Guevara are key documents in the history of the Cuban Revolution. Their writings follow the pattern established by the two previous major communist revolutions, for Stalin—once victory had been consolidated—proceeded to rewrite universal history in terms of the experience of Russia's Communist Party, and Mao did likewise for the Chinese party. Now Guevara, and more recently Debray, are reinterpreting traditional communist doctrine, and it is their "revisions" that have evoked the wrath of conventional communists. And because Debray and Guevara have revised traditional communist doctrine to conform with the actualities of Cuba's past and present, let us now examine these actualities.

Ever since Castro's movement started 14 years ago, the Communist Party has played an ancillary role. As an ideology, Castroism began with a charismatic leader and a band of dedicated nationalists. It moved from that point to a series of insurrectionary successes, which compelled the leader to form a movement—the 26th of July Movement. Then came victorious revolt, which ultimately compelled him to form a party, the Communist Party. The corresponding organizational stages were

■ The prerevolutionary phase (1953-59), during which Castro's politics operated outside the communist movement and its bureaucracy;

■ The united-front stage (1959-62), when the communists from the urban centers and the revolutionaries from the rural sectors were fused into the *Organizaciones Revolutionarias Integradas;*

■ The popular-class stage (1962-65), as Cuba came to be ruled by socialist-Marxist ideology; and

■ The communist stage (1965-   ), during which the name of the party was changed to "Partido Comunista de Cuba." Internal organizational strife, it is true, speeded the attainment of this most recent stage. Still, it is clear that the Partido Comunista de Cuba is a direct reflection of Castro's will and charismatic authority. Domestically, during this stage the old-line Cuban communist leaders were purged; internationally, this stage witnessed Cuba's ideological separation from old-line Latin American communist parties. And this separation constitutes the substance of the Cuban "revolution in the revolution," positing a commitment not merely to the Cuban Revolution, but to a revolution throughout Latin America.

The break with the old-line communist parties, as well as the commitment to a concept of permanent revolution, were demanded by the dynamics of Cuban society—and by the original ideals of the Cuban Revolution.

After the 26th of July Movement had crushed the forces of Batista, the new regime quickly became committed to

Marxism-Leninism and to Soviet patronage. Next, Cuban politics took a nationalistic, inner turn: The Fidelistas would consolidate their power, while building their economy along industrial lines so as to free the nation from her dependence on commodity imports. This course had two grave weaknesses. The attempt at industrialization proved suicidal: Cubans, still dependent upon agriculture, badly needed income from their sugar and tobacco crops. Further, this program of autarchy made in the name of independence in fact threatened to result in Cuba's economic dependence upon the Soviet Union and Cuba's domination by a traditional communist party apparatus.

As early as 1963, when Castro denounced Aníbal Escalante, an old-time Cuban communist and a symbol of old-time Cuban communism, Castro had begun to realize that the old Communist Party constituted an assault upon the ideals of his revolution, and for the following reasons:

■ The centralization of the Communist Party would elevate Havana to a supreme place in the bureaucratic hierarchy, thus depriving Castro of the *rural* mystique so vital to his outlook.

■ The party bureaucracy threatened the charismatic basis of Castro's leadership.

■ If orthodoxy were victorious, Castro would be saddled with not only material but ideological dependence upon the Soviet Union.

■ Orthodox communists threatened Cuba with isolation from other Latin American revolutionaries. Like Stalin, these old-time communists were afraid that every other revolution would be "premature," "lacking in basic historical conditions for change." Finally,

■ Castro felt that orthodoxy would be likely to smother

the revolutionary "will," that human quality that had overcome so many hardships and had actually made the Cuban Revolution possible.

Consequently, Castro felt he had to reinvigorate the revolutionary will. This meant emphasizing the immediate creation of revolutionary situations in the Hemisphere. A new stress was laid on "exporting revolution"—the Cuban model. And the success of this campaign rested upon a rejection of all who challenged the Cuban experience—by treachery, advice, comparison, or any of the tricks played by intellect upon the act. The recalcitrant, orthodox communist machinery was either to be captured by the *guerrilleros,* or—failing this—transcended, bypassed, and even reviled as a nonrevolutionary force.

This new militancy underscores the doctrinal independence of Castro's Communist Party: It is charismatic rather than bureaucratic. This is the ineradicable heritage of the days in the Sierra Maestra mountains. Guerrilla activity gave Castro faith in will rather than in doctrinal blueprints. "The school of war," Fidel told farm-machine workers on Feb. 20, 1967, "taught us how men can do many things, how they can accomplish many tasks when they apply themselves in a practical way. This was the school of war, where a small nucleus of combatants developed into an army without bureaucracy. Without bureaucracy! It went to war, waged war, and won the war without bureaucracy. . . . And war taught us what man can do when he dedicates himself to working with enthusiasm, interest, and common sense."

The revolution in the revolution is also meant to describe the revolutionizing of party organization, for in Cuba the traditional communist order of priorities has been transformed. As Régis Debray formulates it, there must first be the guerrilla group; second, the ripened social class; and only third will there be the authentic revolutionary party. The guerrilla movement is the party apparatus in gestation. In March of this year, Castro defined the party's prime goal: "To us the international communist movement is in the first place just that: a movement of communists, of revolutionary fighters. And those who are not revolutionary fighters cannot be called communists. We conceive of Marxism as revolutionary thinking and action." Castro has thus found a way to differentiate his brand of communism from European and Asian modes—without going outside the framework of Marxism. The Fidelistas have made it clear that Marxism is the *heuristic principle for making revolution,* rather than what lies at the end of the revolutionary rainbow.

But how does one build a new political party? Clearly the mass base, the popular front, the urban compromises, the bait dangled before representatives from all social sectors—the features common to the organizational base of the conventional communist party—all these are anathema to the Fidelistas. For them, the traditional bureaucratic communist party can be a downright liability, frustrating rather than fomenting revolutionary action. In this sense, the current stress on rural revolution abroad may turn out to be Castro's last hurrah—the final settlement of accounts and the ultimate nostalgic bow to the new generation. The question is, Can the revolution survive its own faith in its adolescence?

What this would require, in part at least, is the retention of the heroic image of the Cuban Revolution. That revolution and the Chinese are the two outstanding indigenous socialist revolutions in the post-World War II era. Each, by virtue of its autonomy, felt under few constraints to the Soviet model of 50 years ago. Consequently, Castro's revolution in the revolution goes beyond rebellion against the orthodox dominion of the communist party. It is an all-out effort to use the communist party and the communist ideology as a springboard for recruiting activists. In this sense, the pained if sterile cries of the communists that the Cuban revolutionaries are urging the "liquidation" of the party are right. If the party is to become the refuse heap of the old and the infirm, if it is to give up its manliness, then Castro will indeed enforce its liquidation.

Castro's unconventional view of time and age has led him to other revisions farther and farther from the Marxist-Leninist doctrines. Lurking in the background is what Debray posits as a Manichaean struggle between "socialist guerrillas" (the good guys) and "political commissars" (the bad guys). Debray's juxtaposition is sharper than any made by either Castro or Guevara, but all three support this heresy.

As long as economic conditions in Latin America continue as they are now, or deteriorate relative to the United States and Western Europe, Castro's insurrectionary romanticism, his idealization of will over ideas, will displace the traditional communist long-range view that ultimate victory is expressed by history rather than action: a faith in the ultimate deterioration of the capitalist economy and in the long-range tendencies of capitalist nations to conflict with one another. The short range is thus an expression of discontent with and disbelief in the "historically determined" processes assumed to guide society. The long-range view, that history determines structural change, becomes suspect—as if history itself is a cloak for cowardice and inaction.

A counterpart of Castro's unorthodox position on determinism versus free will is found in the problem of the relationship between his person and the party. For although his rule is undoubtedly based on overwhelming popular support, he must still face the problem of succession—of the transfer of power from self to society. Sporadically during the past two years, Castro has announced that in the future the mass slogan will be transformed from "Everyone with Fidel" to "Everyone with the Party." This is one transformation that has not taken place. Because Castro is still relatively young (40), the matter is eased but not eliminated. The legitimacy of the revolution requires some demonstration of the capacity of the social system to survive the original revolutionary group. It requires that some decision-making machinery be set up. This has not yet been forthcoming; instead, the Fidelistas have launched sustained attacks on the rational decision-making machinery of conventional communist parties.

The specter of personalism, *caudillismo,* continues to haunt the Cuban Revolution, and in this sense Fidel's role is rooted in Latin American tradition. For the *caudillo*— the boss of a province who angles, often successfully, to become dictator of the nation—is the Latin American embodiment of personalism. This in itself is a form of the love-hate relationship of serfs in bondage to the chief (or *jefe*) who played an essential role in the transition from pre-industrial to modern societies. The Cuban Revolution was a military revolution and required the *caudillo* figure to offset the traditional role of the regular army. A good case can be made that this kind of leadership was indispensable in the context of Cuba, which is undergoing socioeconomic transformations not unlike those sponsored by the more "enlightened" *caudillos* of past times, such as Obregón in Mexico or Quiroga in Argentina. But if the 19th century *caudillo* had contempt for the masses he served and remained responsive to the machinations of the middle-class parties, the new-style *caudillo* has only love for the masses and seeks to eradicate the apparatus of electoral politics merely because it is cumbersome.

A symptom, if not a consequence, of *caudillismo* is the rather widespread existence of nepotism throughout the governing ranks. This is especially characteristic of Castro. In picking political leaders, he leans heavily toward long-time cronies and familial contacts. Because of his brother Raúl's steady rise to power (following his appointment in 1959 as heir to the leadership) and the influence of other members of Fidel's extended family, he is surrounded with nonthreatening figures.

The *caudillo* spirit in Latin America has traditionally served to enhance the leader's direct link to the people. In Fidel's case it enables him to bypass, when necessary, the only stable "bureaucratic" apparatus remaining in the country—the Communist Party. Castro even has his alter ego in the post of President—Osvaldo Dorticós—much as Stalin could boast of his in the person of Kliment Voroshilov. The trusted political lieutenant serves to legitimize the remarks of the *caudillo*.

Castro's tendency to nepotism reveals itself most decisively in his humiliation of old-line associates and in his replacing them either with himself or with nonentities. The family power held by Fidel Castro, Raúl Castro, and Vilma Espín (Raúl's wife) cannot be underestimated. Raúl and Vilma, along with Dorticós and Juan Almeida (an old Sierra Maestra companion, now Minister of Labor), are about the most visible leaders in the new Cuba. This is the politics of the purge, the dismemberment of any possible opposition. The purging of a score of veteran Cuban Communist Party leaders—including Aníbal

Escalante, Joaquín Ordoqui, Edith García Buchaca, Juan Marinello, Manuel Luzardo, and Lázaro Peña—had nothing to do with their competence, but simply with their politics. One of the inner-directed aspects of the revolution in the revolution is the elimination of the old party cadre. The ouster of Carlos Rafael Rodríguez as head of the National Institute of Agrarian Reform (I.N.R.A.) in 1965 is the best example of the nexus between personal style and potential ideology. The fact that Castro himself assumed this post is a sign of his increasing concentration of power in himself.

Further, the appointment of a guerrilla cohort—Major Raúl Curbelo, Chief of the Air Force—as Vice President of I.N.R.A. is only one instance of the continued militarization of Cuban society. Only Brazil has a larger army, and only the combined strength of the Argentine armed forces equals the regular armed force size of Cuba. The fusion of personal and political aspects of behavior has served to justify an increased politicization of the military and, no less, of the diplomatic corps. The replacement of the Army Chief of Staff, Armed Forces Vice Minister, Commander of the Navy, and leading officials in the Foreign Ministry represents not simply a tightening of the political net but an increased penetration by the *Líder Máximo* (Maximum Leader) into middle echelons of power. With each series of dismissals, the actual power lodged in civilian agencies seems to become correspondingly weaker; the replacements are less able (or willing) to make decisions independently. Thus, the general militarization of the Hemisphere has had its Left-wing reflex in Cuba.

For the Hemisphere, in turn, these transformations evoke their own terrors. Since it is the impression of most foreign observers that Cuba today is being placed on a wartime footing and is in a state of permanent mobilization, the external ramifications of the revolution in the revolution cannot be dismissed casually.

Restlessness and righteousness have undoubtedly combined to produce the new look in Cuba's foreign policy: the abandonment, to a large extent, of the prudence or caution Castro practiced in the 1962–66 period. This transformation represents responses on three distinct levels:

■ Castro's realization of the dangers attendant on conservatism and bureaucracy, which could obstruct efforts to consolidate the Cuban Revolution.

■ The frustration stemming from Cuba's Hemispheric isolation. Indeed, the list of military-sponsored, Right-wing *golpes de estado (coups d'état)* since 1959 is awesome. And third,

■ The international crisis created by the Vietnam conflict.

The first problem is largely a domestic concern, and it has been dealt with above in terms of Cuba's internal contradictions. It remains only to add that, when Castro threw out prudent foreign policy, he also threw out the baby. The nation-building phase in Cuba came to an end in 1966, and with it ended a certain belief in the viability of a strictly Cuban solution.

In the first years after the Cuban Revolution, its leadership went through the euphoric phase of thinking that Latin American social revolution was on the march. In a sense, the Fidelistas behaved much like the Leninists following their victory after the conclusion of World War I. So certain were the Leninists that the revolution would spread at least to Germany that they made no contingency plans for problems that might emerge from a frustration of communist ambitions. The collapse of international communism in the 1920's helps explain Stalin's single-minded foreign policy. The similar collapse of Latin American communism in the 1960's helps to explain Castroism. For up to 1966, Castro seemed bound by a similar belief that the Cuban revolutionary model projected a unique radiant energy that would power other Hemispheric revolutions.

Yet during this time, the Cuban revolutionaries helplessly watched the utter disarray of Latin America's Leftists. In 1964, Goulart's Brazil went down to crashing counterrevolutionary defeat, and in 1965 Cuba could not mount even a token effort to prevent the Dominican Republic from being restored to a former Trujillo henchman. Throughout Latin America, the image of a mighty torrent of 200 million oppressed peons crushing all obstacles flickered and faded.

Nevertheless, Guevara and his disciples continued to press for total revolution in the Hemisphere. In 1964, Guevara made his "Colonialism Is Doomed" speech before the United Nations. He warned of a "wave of heightened fury, of just demands, of rights that have been flouted, which is rising throughout Latin America." Even after Che left Castro's side, in 1965, the assault on nation-building continued, and by 1966 any strict tendencies toward internal economic development had been repudiated.

In some measure the new turn in Cuban ideology, away from nation-building to continental communism, represents the politics of desperation. For while there are hundreds of thousands of students and workers who share the Cuban perspective, the guerrillas throughout Latin America cannot be numbered even in the thousands. *The New York Times* places the figure at about 750 men. Further, no governments have fallen as a result of the guerrilla activities. In fact, in Colombia, Bolivia, and Venezuela, the guerrilla menace has boomeranged, producing a united front from above—an opposition fusion of military and civilian sectors otherwise often at odds. If this lack of revolutionary victories has stirred the Cubans and their followers to new heights of forensics, it has also, and more substantially, permitted the old-line communists to announce the "bankruptcy" of the new turn.

Castro's retort to these frustrations throughout the Hemisphere constitutes the second level of the transformation of his foreign policy. Its organizational expression is the Organization of Latin American Solidarity, an obvious response to the Organization of American States, from which Cuba was expelled three years after the revolution. This expulsion, taken enthusiastically by the foreign ministers of the United States and reluctantly by those of Latin American states, isolated Cuba solely from the *governments* of other Hemispheric nations—and did that only partially. The governments of Canada and Mexico continued to maintain diplomatic and trade relations with Cuba, and all sorts of private organizations and institutions elsewhere in the Hemisphere continued to provide Cuba with Hemispheric links. Indeed, special tours from Montevideo to Havana are constantly arranged despite the absence of formal diplomatic ties. There is, in fact, a dramaturgical conflict between government and people, with the Castro forces in the vanguard of the latter.

What cannot be lost sight of is that the very existence of the O.A.S. serves to legitimize the O.L.A.S. If an organization can be used for the sole effective purpose of preventing "communist penetration" of the Hemisphere, as is indicated by the Declaration of Caracas, then on a *quid pro quo* basis there is no reason why a parallel organization to rid the Hemisphere of "imperialism" should not also be set up. The O.L.A.S.'s ambiguous situation arises from the fact that the United States is the acknowledged leader of the O.A.S., though whether this leadership function is welcomed by the Latin Americans or imposed upon them is a moot point. But Cuba has not even been accepted as the leader of the Latin American revolutionary forces. And given Cuba's dependent economic status and diminutive size, it is hard to imagine that Castro can impose the same sort of authority on the "communists" of the Hemisphere as the United States can on its "capitalists." This is a clear example of the price paid for having the first socialist revolution in the Hemisphere conducted by one of its smallest nations.

But Castro still holds a few trump cards—one of them, the simple fact that he has made a socialist revolution in an underdeveloped nation. What characterizes revolutions in underdeveloped areas is their discontinuities with the European experience, and even more with the North American experience. The prevailing political framework in Latin America is a juridical delight, a world of laws and orders that employs the forms of constitutionalism without realizing the substance of democratic politics. From the days of the Spanish viceroys, leaders were men who made rules, not those who abided by them. Despite their access to power, the Latin American middle classes have failed to convert their political compassion into affluence for all. Therefore, Castro attacks all sectors of society—including the communists—that affirm their devotion to European political traditions without a corresponding reformation of the social structure.

Régis Debray flatly admits that the bourgeoisie cannot be challenged on the electoral terrain with any hope of victory—at least not in the majority of Latin American countries. In such circumstances, armed struggle must replace parliamentary cretinism. This is the "new dialectic" to which the revolution in the revolution has given rise. "It is possible," Debray declares, "to move from a military *foco* ["center of operations," or focus] to a political *foco,* but to move in the opposite direction is virtually impossible." Debray points out that, expressed schematically, the fundamental lesson of the Cuban Revolution is that it represents the progression "from the military *foco* to the political movement." Thus, at the ideological level the revolution in the revolution represents the transformation of guerrillas into *gorilas,* into advocates of the total militarization of Latin America. This seems to incorporate Rightist doctrine into a Leftist framework. Indeed, for Debray, the physical symbol of the new Left is the military tunic; his heroes, in addition to Fidel, are Ho Chi Minh, Mao Tse-tung, and Ernesto Guevara. But is not the physical representation of the old Right also the military tunic?

There is no plausible reason for equating fascism with Castroism. But the fusion of militarism with revolutionary minoritarianism has no more place in it for classical socialist politics than it has for classical bourgeois politics. Actually, the revolution in the revolution is not so much a call for sheer militancy or a reflection of new class alignments as it is a call for the primacy of the military.

Debray calls the primacy of the military *foco* a "classic involution." However, what it more nearly represents is a return to the politics of radical irrationalism characteristic of French insurrectionary socialism from Babeuf to Sorel. The present stage of the Cuban Revolution represents an unparalleled romantic outburst, but this is very much in keeping with the Latin (French as well as Spanish) ethos. Its romanticism is certified by dead heroes—young soldiers who did not fade away, but died or were captured by the enemy (as Debray was). It is intellectually and emotionally underwritten by a Marxism of free will to replace the Marxism of historical determinism. Real men instead of impersonal man once again make history. This exaltation of flesh-and-blood heroes comes through most clearly in remarks published in the magazine *Tricontinental,* in April 1966, and attributed to Guevara: Tribute is paid to the "martyrs, who will figure in the history of Our America as having given their necessary quota of blood in this last stage of the fight for the total freedom of man."

The resurrection as well as the death is also certified by individuals. As Castro noted earlier this year:

The active mobilization of the people creates new leaders; César Montes and Yon Sosa raise the flag of battle in Guatemala; Fabio Vázquez and Marulanda in Colombia; Douglas Bravo in the western half of the country and Américo Martín in El Bachiller direct their respective fronts in Venezuela. New uprisings will take place in these and other countries of Our America, as has already happened in Bolivia; they will continue to grow in the midst of all the hardships inherent in this dangerous profession of the modern revolutionary.

The case of Yon Sosa demonstrates how even the concept of romanticism has been transformed by Castro in line with his new turn in ideology. At his closing address to the January 1966 Tri-Continental Conference, Castro devoted considerable time to a critique of Yon

Sosa's conduct in Guatemala. He charged that Yon Sosa was a romantic; he did not know revolutionary strategies; he did not know how to win the people. He had allowed himself to be captured by agents of imperialism, by Trotskyites. Ironically enough, Castro's attack was not much different from the attacks the official Communist Party of Cuba made against Castro himself when he was a guerrilla leader in the mountains.

The man Castro defended at the Tri-Continental meeting was Luis Augusto Turcios, who represented Guatemala. Turcios was upheld by Castro as the proper sort of guerrilla revolutionary, a believer in the national rather than in the socialist character of revolution. Since Turcios' death late in 1966, however, criticism of Yon Sosa has been muted, and (as we have seen) this year the Cuban regime restored him to leadership status—in the interests of a common Latin American revolutionary front. Nothing could better indicate the militant turn in Cuban foreign policy.

Cuban romanticism is partially a function of the scale of the revolution and of the nation. Castro today repeatedly harks back to the simpler, purer air of the Sierra Maestra, where an inspired handful of men came down from the mountains to defeat the Goliath in Havana. In assuming the spiritual leadership of the Hemisphere, Castro almost makes a nostalgic appeal for his adherents to go tell it on the mountains. Speaking to Lee Lockwood, a U.S. photographer and journalist, earlier this year, Castro said:

. . . Had we been men with little faith in the Revolution we would have given up the fight following our first setback at the Moncada Garrison [in July 1953], or when our litle army landed from the *Granma* [the boat Castro used in December 1956 for his landing from Mexico] only to be dispersed three days later, and only seven of us were able to reunite. Thousands or rather millions of reasons could have been used as a pretext to say that we were wrong, and that those who said that it was impossible to fight that army, those great forces, were right. However, three weeks later, on January 17, we who at the end of December had barely reunited our forces carried out our first successful attack on an army post, killing its occupants.

In the same vein, Debray expresses the romantic revolutionary irrationale in claiming that "For a revolutionary, failure is a springboard. As a source of theory it is richer than victory. It accumulates experience and knowledge." The young French philosopher clearly learned his lessons well from such irrationalist radical predecessors as Sorel, Peguy, and Bergson. He is, in fact, more a product of *fin de siècle* France than post-revolutionary Cuba.

Of course, Castro has been forced to convert his liabilities into assets, and he has done so very shrewdly. An irreversible fact that he must contend with is Cuba's physical limitations. The major socialist revolutions in Europe and Asia were concluded within the largest land masses in the world (Russia and China). Each had the potential for economic independence, for sustained take-off, for inducing a restructuring of the economic balance of power within their respective spheres of influence. But what could Cuba, the first socialist revolutionary regime in Latin America, do on this score? She was a debtor nation; she could offer no viable economic assistance to revolutionary regimes in trouble.

Paradoxically enough, while Cuba's smallness may be a liability as far as her revolutionary potential is concerned, she has retained intact her function as an exemplary case of a nation breaking her links with the colonial past.

But this is a two-edged weapon. The Cuban leadership tends to underestimate the fact that a model for revolutionaries can also serve as a warning for the established order. In fact, the United States has already stepped up its counterrevolutionary programs in the Hemisphere. And the absence of socialist victories since the Cuban Revolution can scarcely be dismissed as happenstance.

But the happenstance that the first socialist system in the Western Hemisphere has been organized in one of the smallest and least representative nations has clear consequences in political cost accounting. It has raised the cost of revolutions anywhere else. Revolution has become more "expensive" in every other country of the Americas at the very time that the impotence of the first socialist republic became manifest.

In this equation, the United States's intervention in the Dominican Republic in 1965 paid dividends. It unmistakably informed the Latin American nations that the North Americans were in Santo Domingo; the Cubans were not. Nor could they come. Through this action the United States succeeded in defining the Cuban Revolution as something less than a total Latin American revolution. That lesson was not lost. Quite the contrary. Schisms and splits erupted throughout the rest of Latin America, particularly within Cuba.

In Castro's reaction to the stinging taunts about his inaction during the Dominican crisis, righteousness was the keynote. In 1966 he attacked guerrilla insurgents throughout Latin America. In 1967 he generalized his attacks, challenging the right of major non-Hemispheric communist nations, as well as of communist parties in the Hemisphere, to dictate the character of resistance to the United States. In attacking other communist parties, Castro made it plain that their right of leadership had been abrogated. Here restlessness at his own impotence began to seep in. Cuba now proclaimed herself the unique model for guiding revolutionary destinies in resisting the United States. In this way Cuba laid the groundwork for a position as a Third Force within the communist world and within the Third World—a grandiose ideological presumption that again takes advantage of the very smallness of Cuba's base, geographically, demographically, and economically. For underlying this presumption is the profound conviction that Big Power communism is also Big Power chauvinism. The highhanded conduct of the Soviet Union during the missile crisis is a sore point in Cuba today. This is plain in Castro's statement to Lee Lockwood earlier this year:

> Khrushchev had made great gestures of friendship toward our country. He had done things earlier that were extraordinarily helpful to us. But the way in which he conducted himself during the October crisis was to us a serious affront. . . . After the missile crisis, while the Soviet Union was pressing for the withdrawal of the remaining Soviet military personnel in Cuba, the subversive activities of the United States were growing increasingly frequent. In Central America a series of bases had been organized in order to promote aggressions against us. All of which, from our point of view, justified the position we had taken at the beginning of the crisis. . . . The subsequent climate of distrust [between Khrushchev and Castro] could never be completely overcome.

This "climate of distrust" is even more overt in Castro's attitude toward China, despite the many surface resemblances between the two countries. In its first phase, Castro's critique of the Chinese Communist Party could be viewed as a rejection of both foreign domination and also of any unnecessary foreign entanglements. Today, Cuba believes that China also represents Big Power chauvinism.

The basic dilemma of the Cuban revolution in the revolution is whether communism is a national movement or an international movement. Now, for the orthodox communist parties, China's ideological approach represents not Stalinism but Trotskyism. This schism has in fact plagued communism from the first days of its success. At the start of World War I, German and French socialists were faced with a choice between working-class solidarity and nationalism. Naturally, they chose nationalism. A decade later, the Russian Bolsheviks had to choose between "socialism in one country" (the nationalist focus on building and industrializing) and "permanent revolution" (based on the notion of the international solidarity of workers). The path chosen was the former—Stalin's road. Leon Trotsky, the Gray Eagle of the Revolution, was sent into ignominious exile.

The Chinese Revolution has been facing much the same dilemma, but in this case the outcome remains unclear. The young and the old revolutionaries have forged a united front against the Soviet-trained, nation-building, middle-aged generation. Since the old and the young have the upper hand now, China supports the necessity of world revolution—not just of any revolution, but of socialist revolution.

From the orthodox ideological point of view, Castro's attack on China may seem yet another attack on Trotskyism, in its most "insidious" form—Chinese communism. But from the perspective of the recent internal transformation of Cuban ideology, it is an attack on Big Power chauvinism, its rationale and its revolutionary pretenses. From this, even the potential perpetual revolution of the Chinese is not exempt. Then too, one cannot forget that Cuba's bitter assaults on China date from the time it became clear that China could not fulfill her promises of lavish aid.

However severe Cuba's attacks on China are, of course, they are caresses compared with the attacks on "Yankee imperialists." Régis Debray has again made the official formulation: "No one can avoid seeing that in Latin America today the struggle against imperialism is decisive. If it is decisive, then all else is secondary." What is painfully absent from Debray's work, and from any Cuban pronouncements, is any operational analysis of what "imperialism" is all about. It is almost as if subtlety and sophistication would jeopardize the single-minded assault on the enemy.

Cuba has thus carved out for herself a peculiarly Hemispheric role—one in which both Russia and China are denied much of a voice. If the United States defined the Western Hemisphere as off-limits to the European and Asian powers in terms of the Monroe Doctrine, Castro—despite his sensitivity to confrontation—seems to have drawn the same geographic limitations, but in terms of a "Bolívar Doctrine."

In implementing his program for the Hemisphere, Castro faces three essential strategies of change that are now current in Latin America:

■ The United States's strategy—concentrating on developing a national politics of a multiclass variety.

■ The Soviet model—developing a politics of an industrial-class variety in a predominantly urban setting.

■ The Chinese model—developing politics on the basis of mass peasant movements.

The difference between the first and the second and third is nothing short of a choice between reform and revolution. The second and the third differ in that they are two tactics for making revolution. And any knowledge of socialist history will make clear that, once reformist options have been dismissed, the tactical and strategic disputes between revolutionary factions become awesome and fierce. One need look no further to understand why Corvalán and many other Latin American communist leaders boycotted the O.L.A.S. meeting in the summer.

Castro openly supports the revolutionary guerrillas in Venezuela, Guatemala, and Colombia. At the same time, he makes scarcely veiled attacks on the communist leaderships in these countries. The revolution in the revolution, he notes, "acts within revolutionary forms and respects those forms," but this does not prevent "practice coming first and then theory." This practice demands support for the guerrillas as a prime form of foreign relations. Castro indicates that even diplomatic recognition of other Hemispheric nations will not be forthcoming "until there are revolutionary governments leading those countries."

Castro's relations with other, older communist parties in the Hemisphere reached a boiling point in March. With brimstone and vitriol, he lashed out at the Venezuelan party's rejection of the primacy of the guerrilla tactic as "defeatist." In unmistakable terms, he served notice that he would at no time be bound to a "Rightist, capitulationist current" simply because it is bureaucratically promoted "in the name of the international communist movement." At stake here is not merely the course of Venezuela's revolution. In time-honored communist technique, these words cloak a deeper design. Venezuela serves Castro as a surrogate for expressing not simply his frustration at the inaction of socialism elsewhere in the Hemisphere, but also for expressing his claim to ideological leadership in the Hemisphere.

The bitterness of the exchange reveals with terrible clarity the rapid disintegration of the party monolith in the Hemisphere. The current debate is only the latest episode in the long history of controversy within Latin American communism. In the 1940's and 1950's, the pro-Perón and anti-Perón Communist Party factions in Argentina disputed how the party could exploit the dictator's opportunistic swings between Moscow and Washington. During the Goulart epoch, there was the equally critical antagonism between the Chinese-oriented and the Soviet-oriented wings of the Brazilian party. But the Cuban-Venezuelan competition for loyal revolutionists has an especially acrimonious tone, since it involves the interference of a foreign communist party into the affairs of another communist party. Within the O.A.S., the doctrine of nonintervention has generally paralyzed action—despite fervent arguments by the United States for solidarity. Among communists, sovereignty is no less hotly contested. But once Castro adopts the view that his revolution is only the advanced phalanx of a Hemispheric army, no country is foreign to him, none of his revolutionary activities can be defined as "intervention."

In Castro's attack on the Venezuelans, the Righteous Revolutionary did not even entirely spare his Soviet benefactors: "You see how the Venezuelan puppets talk, with their demands that the U.S.S.R. withdraw from the Tri-Continental organization, that the U.S.S.R. do no less than virtually break with Cuba, the 'dead-end street,' to enter through the wide, expansive, and friendly door of the Venezuelan Government, the Government that has slaughtered more communists than any other on this continent!" Castro then introduced a defiant note: "As for us, we are Marxist-Leninists. Let others do as they please. We will never re-establish relations with such a government!" In an obvious challenge to Soviet leadership, Castro concluded with a barbed understatement: "All is not rose-colored in the revolutionary world. Complaints and more complaints are repeated because of contradictory attitudes. While one country [Rumania] is being condemned for reopening relations with Federal Germany, there is a rush to seek relations with oligarchies of the sort run by Leoni [President of Venezuela] and company. A principled position in everything, a principled position in Asia, but a principled position in Latin America, too."

The Venezuelan Communist Party responded with immediacy and savagery, which can in some measure be attributed to the Soviet Government's certain displeasure at Castro's open and unprecedented challenge to its Latin American policy. Curiously, the Venezuelan response was less a rejoinder than an exposure. Castro, too, was called an opportunist: The Cuban regime, while calling for a "principled" stand in the Hemisphere, trades and carries on diplomatic negotiations with the fascist Franco regime. And, to justify its own position, the Venezuelan Communist Party invoked the classical contest between polity and morality. In 1966 Castro took virtually the same moralistic tack in criticizing China's actions: "From the first moment, we understood the obvious opportunistic position taken by China in trade relationships. . . . A much more important and fundamental question than food is whether the world of tomorrow can assume the right to blackmail, extort, pressure, and strangle small peoples." This year, at Cuba's instigation, the O.L.A.S. meeting adopted an astoundingly harsh resolution condemning the U.S.S.R. and other East European states for trading with the oligarchic regimes of Latin America. These are clearly idiosyncratic Latin American responses, for the accepted role of the sovereign state is to conduct foreign policy in the best interests of its own people. The substitution of moral absolutes for such a practical goal must seem as suicidal to communist politicians as to bourgeois politicians. In sum, the Cuba-Venezuela dispute has tangled somewhat the threads of national self-interest and international solidarity among communists. Ideological disputes are not unresponsive to nationalist sentiments, particularly in Latin America, where such sentiments are powerful among the Left as well as the Right. And if the Fidelistas have moved closer to "permanent" Hemispheric revolution since the Tri-Continental Conference, the Venezuelans, in the wake of their activist guerrilla wing's bitter defeats and the internal disaffiliation of their Armed Forces of National Liberation, have moved further toward intense nationalism and political accommodation.

The tone of the Venezuelan response to Castro makes clear the "classical" nature of the contest. In a sharp rebuke, the response noted that "the aberration in the Castro position is that it makes him unable to pronounce the word 'peace.' It does not constitute a renunciation of any principles to urge the formulation of a democratic peace for Venezuela—particularly at a time when the most rapacious sectors of the ruling class are interested in gathering excuses for a policy of violence, and when a policy of violence has been repudiated by the majority of the country." The Venezuelan party further reasserts the primacy of organization over will: "It is necessary to point out that we are not attempting to provoke communist insurrections or create pure communists. We are attempting to prepare and organize a national revolutionary movement capable of opening new pathways of independent development for our nation. In this sense, it is imperative that the C.P.V. organize a vast movement, with the workers and peasants in a mutually reenforced alliance, which also has the potential for including those sectors of the middle class and those national patriots able and willing to put an end to colonization and underdevelopment." Teodoro Petkoff and his fellow leaders of the C.P.V. put the matter of Cuban assistance bluntly: "We will never accept agents of Cuba in Venezuela—as if they are the only true communist party in the world. We are Venezuelan communists, and we cannot accept tutelage under anybody." The declaration added tauntingly that "if there are small revolutionary groups that are eager to come under the tutelage of Fidel Castro, that is their business, not ours. The C.P.V. will never accept such subordination."

Underneath the rousing rhetoric emanating from Cuba and Venezuela is a sociological disagreement. The orthodox communist position holds that a genuine national politics can emerge only when industrial classes within the cities perceive themselves as linked to the peasant masses in the rural area. It follows that the forces that control the cities control the nation. The catch is that today the aspirations of the organized working classes are much more nearly those of the middle sectors than those of the peasant masses. Urbanization and modernization have cut the ground from under traditional communist prescriptions. In Castro's almost pathological disdain for big-city politics, there is more than a hint of the nostalgic yearning for an age of peasant innocence, untouched by the corruption of the monstrous secular city.

The alternative position presented by Castro is an adaptation from Mao Tse-tung: The peasant mass surrounds the cities and overwhelms the urban-based sectors. At least in the initial guerrilla phase, those who control the rural countryside control the nation. The supreme difficulty of this approach in Latin America is the heavy concentration of the population in the coastal regions—the result of the masses' reliance upon migration rather than insurgency to obtain their goals. Castro's emotional response, inconsistent with his long-run aim of industrialization, is to identify urbanism with bureaucratic corruption.

In many parts of Latin America, moreover, the peasant masses may be unwilling to play their assigned role; many remain so tied to a semifeudal culture that their primary allegiance is to the *latifundistas* (big landowners) rather than to the revolutionaries. The recognition of this social variable by Debray, Guevara, and others has led to a view of guerrilla insurgency as dependent less upon the rural peasant than on the mountain terrain. This shift from a class approach to an ecological approach contributes to making romanticism a far more profound ingredient of present-day guerrilla insurgency in Venezuela, Guatemala, and Colombia than it ever was in the actual forging of the Cuban Revolution. In this sense, the revolution in the revolution can be seen as an attempt to transcend the actual empirical situation and return to the very theorizing Castro shows such contempt for on other grounds.

One more cause of Castro's new boldness in foreign policy is his reaction to the war in Vietnam, a reaction that links his Hemispheric ambitions with his pretensions to Third World leadership. It also brings this small socialist state into a confrontation with the United States. Again it is Che Guevara who announces the theme. In the *Tricontinental* article presumably written by him, he defined Cuba's Third Force approach in relation to Vietnam. He pictured Vietnam as the primary ally of Cuba. As an outpost of socialism in Asia, Vietnam's position is parallel to Cuba's in the Western Hemisphere: "This is the sad reality: Vietnam—a nation representing the aspirations, the hopes of a whole world of forgotten peoples—is tragically alone. . . . The solidarity of all progressive forces of the world with the people of Vietnam today is similar to the bitter irony of the plebeians urging on the gladiators in the Roman arena." Guevara is quite precise on this point. "It is not a matter of wishing success to the victim of aggression, but of sharing his fate; one must accompany him to his death or to victory. When we analyze the lonely situation of the Vietnamese people, we are overcome by anguish at this illogical fix in which humanity finds itself. U.S. imperialism is guilty of aggression—its crimes are enormous and cover the whole world. We already know all that, gentlemen! But this guilt also applies to those who, when the time came for a definition, hesitated to make Vietnam an inviolable part of the socialist world; running, of course, the risks of a war on a global scale, but also forcing a decision upon imperialism. The guilt also applies to those who maintain a war of abuse and maneuvering—started quite some time ago by the representatives of the two greatest powers of the socialist camp."

Guevara then called for many Vietnams throughout Latin America. This exhortation, he asserted, is a consequence of the general impotence and shortcomings of China and the Soviet Union. Unsparingly he described the masculine, apocalyptic warfare and warriors these Vietnams would require: "Relentless hatred of the enemy impels us over and beyond the natural limitations of man and transforms us into effective, violent, selective, and cold killing-machines. Our soldiers must be thus; a people without hatred cannot vanquish a brutal enemy. We must carry the war as far as the enemy carries it: to his home, to his centers of entertainment, in a total war. It is necessary to prevent him from having a moment of peace, a quiet moment outside his barracks or even inside; we must attack him wherever he may be, make him feel like a cornered beast wherever he may move." Guevara concludes with a call to arms: "What a luminous, clear future would be visible to us if two, three, or many Vietnams flourished throughout the world."

Not to be overlooked is the belief shared by the Cuban political leadership that an end to the fighting in Vietnam would signal the beginning of a United States offensive to "rid the Hemisphere of communism." Cuba sees the opening of this crusade in the Venezuelan Government's complaint to the Organization of American States that Castro is supplying and providing men for the anti-Government guerrilla movement.

If the best defense is an offense, then the Cuban leadership is performing correctly. The regime refused to disclaim any knowledge of the three Cubans in a landing party of revolutionists caught by Venezuelan Government forces. Instead, Havana declared on May 18, 1967, that "Cuba is lending and will continue to lend aid to all those who fight against imperialism in whatever part of the world." This commitment, in turn, rests on a profound conviction that a more active insurrectionary role would not harm Cuba—and would probably yield heightened respect in those sectors of the Latin American Left most disillusioned and disheartened by Cuba's prudent response to the U.S. intervention in the Dominican Republic.

The question of morale remains an important constituent of Castro's thinking. Guevara has cautioned: "We must not underrate our adversary; the U.S. soldier has technical capacity and is backed by weapons and resources of such magnitude as to render him formidable. He lacks the essential ideological motivation which his bitterest enemies of today—the Vietnamese soldiers—have in the highest degree." Castro's newly radical foreign policy itself seems to rest on the belief that no matter what the United States-dominated O.A.S. orders, the people of Latin America will never willingly fight Cuba. Furthermore, there is a tacit belief that the Soviet Union will never willingly stop supporting Cuba, at least to the extent of underwriting her sugar crop, no matter how resentful orthodox Latin American communist parties may become—or, for that matter, the Soviet Union itself. It is doubtful whether this will be enough to fuel Castro's ambitions, however. In defending his passivity during the Dominican civil war, Castro pointed out (perhaps inadvertently) the purely defensive nature of the Cuban armed forces: "Cuba has weapons to defend herself, but in relation to the imperialists, they are infinitely inferior. Cuba has defensive arms."

Nevertheless, the new Cuban ideology downgrades the role of weaponry. In the romantic rationale, technology cannot halt the human agent of social change. On April 19, 1967, the sixth anniversary of the Bay of Pigs landing (now a Cuban national holiday), Castro reasserted his willingness to have Cuba serve as the Vietnam of the West, a kind of Second Front within the Third World. Plainly referring to the United States, he warned that "the firepower and combat capacity they would find here is equivalent to more than three times the firepower of the revolutionary combatants of South Vietnam. . . . As to the rest, let them find out for themselves should the time come. The imperialists must confront Vietnam, plus the several Vietnams that are developing on this continent, plus the Vietnam that they are going to find here if they attack us."

Even with the final prudent proviso, "If they attack us," the unabashed and uninhibited defense of guerrilla combat, along with the clear willingness to flout existing diplomatic truces, could well be the opening gambit in a Cuban maneuver to provoke the United States into a line of action that would once and for all crystallize the polarization of the United States and Latin America.

Amazingly, this Cuban programming of U.S. foreign policy may succeed. Castro now seems to have the United States military programmed to adopt a form of precipitate behavior that might well induce a second Vietnam. While on the surface this appears to be a Cuban invitation to attend her own suicide, there are several factors operating for Castro in Cuba that did not exist in any country where the United States previously intervened.

■ Cuba is fully mobilized and prepared, militarily and psychologically, for attack.

■ The Cuban population's support of the regime appears solid enough to rule out the possibility of any immediate collapse of the regime. Finally,

■ In any future invasion, the United States—unlike its hands-off posture in the Bay of Pigs expedition—would have to draw on its own heavily committed armed forces. It could not rely on exiles to perform Hessian services.

If this analysis is correct, then there has been a profound transformation in the Castro regime: not merely an abandonment of the prudent policy that characterized the first eight years of the regime's existence, but—more than that —the possibility of full-scale military operations "only ninety miles from home."

There is monumental tragedy in this prospect—for Castro, for the United States, for the Hemisphere. The revolution within the revolution proposes a transcendence of the party organization through a reassertion of personality. The *true* party, in contrast with the established party, would be manned by symbolic leaders of proved revolutionary capacity, organizing for the great push outward against Big Powers and Big Brothers. At the psychological level, the new turn in Cuban ideology calls for liberation from the dominance of the bureaucratic party and instead the exaltation of the individual. At the political level, the new turn calls for a redefinition of victory as a Hemispheric issue rather than a national issue. Marx observed that when history repeats itself, what was tragedy returns as comedy. In Hemispheric history, under Castro's impact, the classic tragedy of the schism between organization and humanism, internationalism and nationalism, may return not as comedy, but as calamity.

October 1967

FURTHER READING SUGGESTED BY THE AUTHOR:

Studies on Cuba continue to grow, but their quality has declined markedly ever since the inundation of an apologetic and tendentious exile literature. Still, there are a number of recent works in English that deserve careful attention.

Revolution in the Revolution? by Régis Debray (New York: Monthly Review, 1967). The famed study by the French philosopher-guerrilla fighter who has sought to provide ideological backbone to the new turn in Cuban politics.

Castro's Cuba, Cuba's Fidel by Lee Lockwood (New York: The Macmillan Company, 1967). A remarkable set of interviews with Fidel Castro, providing the most up-to-date account of the Cuban Premier's beliefs and attitudes.

Revolutionary Politics and the Cuban Working Class by Maurice Zeitlin (Princeton, N.J.: Princeton University Press, 1967). The first significant sociological field-study of postrevolutionary Cuba. The attitudes of the masses expressed, though based on data obtained in 1962, remain unquestionably correct.

Revolution—
For Internal Consumption
Only

RICHARD R. FAGEN

Many students of the Castro regime, both critics and supporters, devote an inordinate amount of attention to the guerrilla stage of the Cuban experience. The critics fear that violent revolution might sweep like a brushfire through the hemisphere, whereas the supporters argue that armed struggle is the only road to national liberation and development. One consequence of this infatuation with the guerrilla stage is that the lessons to be learned from the study of the first ten years of Castroite rule have been neglected. Moreover, even when they do pay attention to the developmental aspects of the post-guerrilla stage, both the enemies and friends of the revolution have failed to appreciate how profoundly revolutionary programs have been conditioned and shaped by a series of factors that are peculiarly Cuban, factors which set the island apart from much of the rest of Latin America. Because they see armed struggle as either the curse or the hope of the hemisphere, they also see the revolution in power as a foretaste or a blueprint for what another radical regime might be or do. But neglect of the specialness of the Cuban case leads one to overestimate its transfer value and oversimplify the transformations that have taken place. This article is an attempt to rectify that overestimate and the misperceptions that flow from it. Above all, it is argued that the Cuban revolutionary regime has been relatively advantaged in the pursuit of its developmental goals in ways which will not be typical of other radical elites that may come to power in Latin America or the rest of the third world.

Thus, the analysis that follows does not seek to explain *why* the Cuban Revolution occurred in the first place or why it took such radical form once in power. The narrower interest is in the cumulative impact on revolutionary rule and programs of certain features of Cuban society, Castroite leadership, and the world environment. Conditioning factors shaping the Cuban case can be grouped under four headings: sociocultural integration; socioeconomic development and potential; leadership characteristics; and particularities of Cuban history and world politics.

When Castro came to power, Cuba was among the most homogeneous nations in Latin America, Asia, or Africa. Probably no other postwar radical nationalists have been so advantaged as the Cuban in working with a sociocultural system relatively free of divisive cleavages. Cuba had its share of social and economic problems, but it was not a fragmented or agglomerate nation. Elite efforts encountered no obdurate tribal minorities, no separatist territorial factions, no language enclaves, no paralyzing racial problems, no premodern Indian communities. Living on an island without great climatic extremes, no insurmountable geographical barriers, and no overpopulation problem on the horizon, the more than 7 million Cubans presented a striking contrast to countries such as Indonesia or Mexico. Batista's Cuba exhibited a greater degree of national integration than did Mexico after 50 years of "integrative revolution." Such was the sociocultural legacy inherited by Castro. When evaluating the revolutionary system in Cuba, it is necessary to keep this legacy in mind.

The outsider might question this perspective by pointing to the Negro-white cleavage in pre-Castro Cuba. The 1953 census classified 12.4 percent of the population Negro and 14.5 percent mixed race. Many observers contend that the census figures underestimate both the cultural and the physical presence of the Negro. African art forms, vocabulary and blood were diffused through the society to a much greater degree than census statistics indicate. Although no legalized racial segregation existed, there was widespread social and economic discrimination based on custom and usage.

But racial relations were of the Latin rather than the Anglo-Saxon variety. Mulattoes—like Batista—could be found in top political and upper-middle economic positions if not in high society.

Though the man of dark skin was greatly disadvantaged in prerevolutionary Cuba, racial cleavage was not so complete as to constitute an impediment to political mobilization and social transformation after Castro came to power. Rather, although the legacies of Negro culture deprivation linger on, the most serious manifestations of discrimination —social exclusion and lack of equal educational and economic opportunities—were terminated by revolutionary decree. Whatever undercurrents of personal prejudice remain do not find expression in institutionalized discrimination. Thus, the racial problem in Cuba was, if anything, a boon to Castro. In the hands of the revolutionaries, the race issue was extremely useful for discrediting the old social order. Furthermore, because of the "instant liberation" of the Negro, tens of thousands of disadvantaged Cubans were recruited into the ranks of revolutionary enthusiasts.

As Theodore Draper and others have shown, Cuba in the 1950's was far from an underdeveloped country when viewed in world context. No major Asian or African nation, except Japan, enjoyed such an impressive socioeconomic profile. In Latin America, only Argentina, Chile, Uruguay, and occasionally Venezuela topped Cuba.

Table 1 presents eight indices of Cuba's relative socioeconomic position in Latin America about the time Castro came to power. For additional comparisons, the final column indicates in each instance a European nation that was close to but actually *lower than* Cuba on each index.

Statistics of this sort do not, however, tell the whole story. Under the comforting averages and national comparisons could be found a Cuba characterized by vast inequalities in the distribution of goods, services, and opportunities. True, there was one doctor for every 1,000 inhabitants, a figure that compared favorably with that of one doctor for every 760 inhabitants in the United States. True, there were 72 television sets for every 1,000 inhabitants, a figure more impressive than the 57 sets for every 1,000 inhabitants found at the same time in France. But where *were* the doctors and the television sets, or for that matter the schools, the decent housing, and the well-paying jobs? In Havana, of course, and in a few other large urban centers. The countryside, the *campo,* presented a far less attractive picture. Illiteracy, poverty, poor health, and seasonal unemployment were widespread. Few schools, fewer clinics, bad roads, impure water, and little or no electricity characterized the rural landscape. Almost all observers of prerevolutionary Cuba were struck by the contrast between urban and rural areas. The island, if not underdeveloped in the conventional sense, was unevenly and inharmoniously developed in the manner characteristic of many Latin American nations.

Other well known characteristics of the pre-Castro Cuban economy help to explain the inharmonious development:

■ A substantial resource base was only partially exploited and frequently under the control of foreign interests.

■ An agricultural economy largely dependent on sugar was vulnerable to fluctuations in international prices, with production concentrated on large plantations using some modern technology and with a seasonal work force that was unemployed for the rest of the year.

■ Public utilities were dominated by North American con-

CUBA IN SOCIOECONOMIC PERSPECTIVE		Table 1
Variable	Rank in Latin America	Similar European Nation
Gross national product per capita	4th (1957)	Rumania
Commercial energy consumption per capita	6th (1955)	Yugoslavia
Percentage of population literate	5th (1950s)	Yugoslavia
Daily newspaper circulation per 1000 population	4th (1960)	Italy
Radios per 1000 population	2nd (1960)	Italy
Television sets per 1000 population	1st (1961)	France
Students in higher education per 1000 population	7th (1960)	Norway
Inhabitants per physician	3rd (1960)	Sweden

cerns, with American money important but *not* predominant in railways, sugar, and banking.

■ A well-developed urban labor movement, partially captive and corrupt, nevertheless assured its organized segments many work benefits and slowly rising real income.

■ Government intervention in the economy was sporadic and often contaminated by favoritism; there was no national planning or regulation commensurate with the magnitude of existing problems in agriculture, industry, and trade.

Statistics on the Cuban economy, its social consequences, and its potential are typically used in one of two ways.

Opponents of the Castro regime fasten on the data to bolster their claim that Cuba, being quite well developed, did not "need" a revolution, or at least not one as radical as Castro made. However, revolutionaries constantly point to the sharp contrasts on the island itself and to the disparities between the Cuba of Batista and the Cuba that "might have been." The coexistence of impressive resources and extensive poverty, modern cities and rural underdevelopment, has been used from the beginning by the revolutionaries to give bite to their charge that Cuba was "a rich land inhabited by impoverished people." But the statistics can also be used in a third way, less dramatic but ultimately more useful for analysis.

Despite disagreement about particulars, three general characteristics of pre-Castro socioeconomic development can be agreed upon. First, many of the human and material resources necessary for a national developmental effort could be found in the urban and industrial base, in the economic structure of transportation and communication and in the manpower pool. Second, the discontinuities and inconsistencies in the socioeconomic fabric were large enough to trigger and justify such a national effort. Third, the depressed sectors of the society were not sufficiently isolated either geographically or culturally from the more advanced sectors so as to render difficult or impossible the penetration of the former by the latter. For example, Sidney W. Mintz states, "A very substantial part of the Cuban rural labor force was a proletariat, but a rural proletariat: landless, propertyless, wage-earning, and store-buying." Clearly, this type of rural proletariat, although poor, is already "modern" and therefore available to the planners in a way that an isolated, Indian, subsistence-farming peasantry is not.

After taking power, the urban-based revolutionaries declared war on the countryside and socioeconomic backwardness in general. They controlled the men, materials, and political support necessary to initiate the war. They faced enemies—hunger, disease, illiteracy—real enough and evil enough to make the war both self-evident and popular. It is entirely possible that this attack by the developed sector on the under-developed sector has been strategically and tactically mismanaged. In practice it has sometimes been organizationally inept, economically wasteful, and ideologically perverse. In the larger context of Cuban socioeconomic development, however, the decision to declare war was neither unrealistic nor rash. On the contrary, economic and moral criteria argued that the effort could and should be made. The question was, how and by whom? Castro and his lieutenants supplied the will and the plan, but many of the resources and all of the problems were a legacy from Batista and his predecessors.

The counterpoint of wealth and poverty, development and underdevelopment, aids in placing Castroite revolutionary efforts in perspective. The regime fell heir to socioeconomic problems of large enough scale to anger the egalitarians, challenge the technocrats, and mobilize the citizens. The regime also fell heir to substantial socioeconomic resources that gave real hope of massive accomplishments within one generation. The reformer's pledge, "Our children shall live better than we," had a meaning in Cuba that it could not possibly have in Guinea or Burma or even in Guatemala. The same resource base which gave credibility to open-ended radical promises lent support to specific revolutionary programs. For instance, a massive campaign to eradicate illiteracy and educate citizens in a country already enjoying 75 percent literacy and a highly developed mass media system has a ring of realism about it that is lacking in similar campaigns undertaken in nations still predominantly illiterate and preindustrial.

All students of Cuba are in agreement on one essential: for better or for worse, the revolution bears the indelible imprint of one man—Fidel Castro. This does not make the last decade of Cuba's history any easier to understand, for

Castro himself allows no easy interpretation. He is, as many have noted, very intelligent, energetic, proud, an astute politician and a gifted orator. On the other hand, he has yet to prove himself either an able administrator or a realistic economist. Seemingly without interest in material gain, intolerant of self-indulgence in others, he is relentless in his pursuit of political power. While hardly consistent over the years in some of his policies and public pronouncements, he has been *extremely* consistent in reasserting his dominance over the shifting revolutionary power structure. He moved with vigor and skill against dissidents within his organization, and later challenged and defeated the old-line Cuban Communists when they tried to usurp control of the new Marxist-Leninist coalition that he had put together. And he has certainly not proved an easy man for other world leaders, either Soviet or American, to manage.

For an understanding of political mobilization and social transformation in Cuba, the most important attribute of Castro is his charisma. Strictly speaking, this is not a characteristic of the man himself, but of his relationship with the masses. Following the well-known formulation by Max Weber, charisma involves much more than popularity. The charismatic leader is perceived by his followers as being endowed with superhuman or at least exceptional powers or qualities. And he perceives himself as "elected" from above to fulfill a mission. Both of these requirements were met in Cuba. Although time and the exigencies of rule have undoubtedly eroded Castro's charisma, he still commands an impressive and devoted following on the island. The call to associate oneself with Fidel and through him with the miracle of the *Granma*, the glories of the Sierra Maestra, the defeat of Batista, the victory of Playa Girón, and the transformation of the social order continues to stir the Cuban masses in a way not easily understood by those who have not lived through the events. For many, the revolution remains incarnate in Fidel, and his right to command remains unquestioned. He is the prophet who led his people out of the Batista wilderness, turned back the Yankee hordes, and is constructing a promised land. of full employment and social equality. A legend before his 33rd birthday and the maximum leader ever since, Castro's presence—both physical and symbolic—has been a key element in all revolutionary programs undertaken in the new Cuba.

Taken one at a time, none of the characteristics of Castro is exceptional. Gandhi was probably as complex, Nkrumah perhaps as charismatic in the early years, Mao certainly as astute and successful in consolidating power during the first half decade, and Nasser as fortunate in seizing and exercising control over a relatively undamaged society. But the gestalt is uniquely Cuban. The stamp of Castro is on the Cuban effort. It could not be otherwise, for Fidel dominates the revolution. He is Sidney Hook's "event-making man" par excellence.

In part because of the *personalismo* and charisma of Castro, and in part because of his political audacity and effectiveness, Cuba has not been torn by intraelite struggles of a paralytic sort. It should be noted that there *has* been infighting: moderates against radicals, communists against noncommunists, new Marxists against old Marxists, followers of Peking against followers of Moscow. What has not occurred, however, is internal strife of sufficient magnitude to either dislocate or overturn the top leadership. Castro is still number one, Dorticós is still President. Second-level revolutionaries, such as Armando Hart and Juan Almeida, have been active and faithful since the first rebels landed in Cuba late in 1956. The catalog of early revolutionaries and second-generation militants now alienated is also long. But none of these potential counterelites organized a sustained and effective opposition to Castro. Now they are silenced, in exile, in prison, or in some cases dead.

The continuity in top leadership has eased the implementation of revolutionary programs. First, since 1959 no dramatic interruptions or reversals have occurred in the content of the programs. There were no new elites in power, bent on denying the legitimacy and even the existence of their predecessors. Nor was there any organized opposition of sufficient strength to communicate to a mass audience a revolutionary (or counterrevolutionary) vision challenging Castro's. Second, the limited nature of the struggle against Batista and the absence of disruptive civil strife since that time have left Cuba with its socioeconomic resource base relatively intact. The largest single loss has come through the outpouring of exiles possessing technical and social skills. But, as Castro has pointed out, the flight of the exiles may be a blessing. Exiles take with them needed skills, but their departure also "purifies" and strengthens the movement by removing those of questionable loyalty while enriching government coffers with confiscated lands and goods.

Although the damages incurred by Cuban civil strife from 1953 to 1963 may seem immense to those close to the revolution, comparing the Cuban case with the Mexican achieves some perspective. In 1920, at the end of a decade of internal struggle, Mexico had paid dearly. Madero, Huerta, Zapata, Carranza, and hundreds of thousands of others were dead. Many farms were untended or in ruins, transportation and communication were disrupted. Industry was just beginning to recover from damages. Moreover, powerful opposition leaders, commanding substantial economic and political resources, continued to threaten the government in power. Compared with this decade of turmoil, the Cuban experience seems mild. The revolutionary leadership consolidated and maintained its hold on society with considerable ease, capturing almost intact the socioeconomic resources of the island and expending little energy on the suppression of civil strife. Resources were invested almost immediately in the work of social transformation and there they have remained ever since.

Unlike continental Spanish America, freed from colonial rule by the Creole revolts of the 1820's, Cubans continued under Spanish domination until the end of the 19th century. In the latter half of that century, there was a series of Cuban protests and rebellions against Spain and the institutions of slavery. The Ten Years' War of 1868 to 1878 and the War of 1895 are the two historical and symbolic high-water marks of this period, but anti-Spanish and anti-colonial activity was almost continuous. Names such as Carlos Manuel de Céspedes, the wealthy planter who fought in the Ten Years' War, Máximo Gómez and Antonio Maceo, the two great generals of the epoch, and José Martí, poet, politician, rebel, and military strategist, head the list of late 19th century nationalist heroes. Interrupted by American intervention, this relatively recent flowering of national independence and identity in Cuba sets the background against which the 20th century drama of nationalism and revolution was played.

From the revolutionary and nationalistic viewpoint, the tangled and passionate web of Cuban-American relations in the first six decades of the 20th century is an asset. Apologists for the Cuban side cite chapter and verse to substantiate their claim that for 60 years the United States controlled the politics, plundered the resources, humiliated the population and crippled the economy of the island. Defenders of United States policy list manifold social and economic benefits that Cubans accrued during the American presence. But for our purpose it is not necessary to attempt a detailed reconciliation of these two extreme interpretations of history. Consistent with both are three key assertions. First, the degree of American political involvement in Cuba was considerable. The Platt Amendment, in effect from 1901 to 1934, stated that "Cuba consents that the United States may exercise the right to intervene for the preservation of Cuban independence, the maintenance of a government adequate for the protection of life, property, and individual liberty." Second, the degree of American economic involvement in Cuba was even greater. Third, without arguing the morality of this political and economic involvement or whether American presence stunted Cuban economic development, it must have been galling for Cuban nationalists to live for 60 years in the political and economic shadow of the United States.

Turning to the Castro period, disintegration of Cuban-American relations was rapid during 1959, the regime's first year in power. By January of 1961, the United States had broken diplomatic relations with Cuba; the Bay of Pigs invasion followed in April. To explain the course of events leading to this antagonism, Cubans cite American opposition to the first agrarian reform and to the later nationalization laws, attacks by Miami-based exiles, the refusal of United States owned refineries to process Soviet crude oil, reduction of the United States quota for Cuban sugar, economic embargo on United States goods shipped to Cuba and espionage and subversion by United States agents. American spokesmen muster an equally long list of Cuban provocations and misdeeds: executions, Communist infiltration in government, expropriation without compensation, destruction of press autonomy, recognition of Communist China, increasing economic dependence on the Soviet bloc, export of revolution to the hemisphere, and attacks on United States officials, citizens, policies, and property. It is clear that an interactive and self-supporting system of threat and counterthreat, misunderstanding and counter-misunderstanding, retaliation and counterretaliation was established between Cuba and the United States in 1959 and 1960. By 1961, the antagonism had congealed. Further moves by both sides, the Bay of Pigs invasion, the embrace of Marxism-Leninism, the missile crisis, United States overflights, and Cuban hemispheric mischief-making only reinforced the hostility.

Undergirding and coloring Cuban interpretations of

these events is a long and complex history of anti-Americanism. Since at least the time of José Martí and the Spanish-American War, antagonism toward the United States was a recurring theme in Cuban politics—although its earlier volume and pervasiveness rarely approached the level attained under Castro after 1960. The most fully institutionalized pre-Castro expression of anti-Americanism came in the first years of the Party of the Cuban Revolution, or *Auténticos,* founded in the 1930's. The 1935 program of the *Auténticos* was organized around the symbolic triumvirate of "nationalism, socialism, and antiimperialism." By nationalism was meant national independence and development. By antiimperialism was meant disengagement from North American political and economic control.

But long before the *Auténticos* began to broadcast their own brand of anti-Americanism, publicly expressed dislike for the "colossus of the North" was heard on the island. In 1922, after developments in the sugar trade and the sugar industry that were considered by many Cubans to be inimical to their interests, one Havana newspaper printed the following banner headline: "Hatred of North Americans Will Be the Religion of Cubans." The paper continued, "The day will have to arrive when we will consider it the most sacred duty of our life to walk along the street and eliminate the first American we encounter."

For the revolutionary, the current struggle thus is rooted in six decades of exploitation, and the millennial order to come is seen as involving the total rejection of the United States, as both mentor and model. Without undue misrepresentation of "the facts," the Cubans can selectively mine the historical record for events and statistics of great evocative power and high credibility. It is a rich treasure indeed. In the hemisphere, only Mexico, Panama, and now perhaps the Dominican Republic can lay claim to such an impressive catalogue of anti-American grievances.

For the Cubans to indulge in a revolutionary effort having virulent anti-Americanism as a prime component is a luxury made possible in part by the Cold War. The point needs little elaboration here. Without the economic umbilical cord linking Cuba to the Soviet Union and much of Eastern Europe, the Castro regime could not survive—at least not in its present form. Before the advent of the Cold War, it would have been impossible for the revolutionary elite to move so radically in either the domestic or the international arena. If the elite violates "laws" of history, geography, and economics and is not brought to a reckoning, it is because under the special circumstances of the 1960's the old "laws" do not always apply.

Nowhere is this seen more clearly than in hemispheric political-military relations. Vulnerable throughout most of the 20th century to incursions by United States money and Marines, Cuba is now well defended. Protected by water, its own armed forces, perhaps by Soviet power and the norms of nonintervention, the regime is relatively well insulated from the threats, border incidents and attacks to which it would otherwise be subjected. Although the island is close enough to the United States—both geographically and historically—to make Castro's expressed fear of the colossus seem reasonable, Cuba is distant enough and visible enough internationally to make effective action *against* the regime both difficult and politically costly. Fortress Cuba can be neither nibbled away nor attacked with traditional prewar impunity. Despite the asymmetry of political and economic power, Cuba can effectively hold the United States at bay while profiting from the symbolic and integrative consequences of the antagonism.

In conclusion, Castro's Cuba is a child both of the times and of the ages—both of the Cold War and of the centuries-old revolutionary tradition. It is a social transformation sufficiently far-reaching to be classified with the French, Mexican, Soviet, and Chinese examples and is also an indigenous movement sufficiently shaped by Cuban history, geography, economy, culture, and personalities to be considered apart. Both perspectives on the revolution, the broadly comparative and the more narrowly particular, contribute to our understanding.

April 1969

FURTHER READING SUGGESTED BY THE AUTHOR:

Castroism: Theory and Practice by Theodore Draper (New York: Praeger, 1965). This is his second criticism of Castroism.

Twentieth Century Cuba: The Background of the Castro Revolution by Wyatt MacGaffey and Clifford R. Barnett (Garden City, N.Y.: Doubleday Anchor, 1965). This is the best one-volume introduction to the nature of Cuban society, polity, and economy when Castro took over.

Background to Revolution: The Development of Modern Cuba by Robert F. Smith (New York: Knopf, 1966) is a useful collection of pre-Castro writings.

Student Power In Action

ARLIE HOCHSCHILD

Cubans use the term "university revolution" to mean something different from the pickets and tear gas now its trademark on American campuses. The Cuban revolution of 1958 turned the University of Havana on its head. Established faculties were dismantled. Professors left and were replaced by students. Transformation of education took place in the time that the University of California at Berkeley spent publishing a report on what should be done about its own troubled campus. Ironically, many recommendations made at Berkeley to establish a sense of community and better student-faculty relations are realities in Cuba, an unintended result of more far-reaching political, economic, and social upheaval. The 27,000 students of the University of Havana complain not of impersonality, lack of community, access to teachers, or the "irrelevance" of what they learn, but of a lack of qualified teachers (three-fourths of the chemistry faculty are students teaching courses they have just passed) and a lack of textbooks in

53

their own language (due to a shortage of paper and of foreign exchange).

In some ways, student generations in the United States have their opposites in Cuba. The Cuban counterpart of the silent fifties on American campuses was an activist generation in which most of the 20,000 people killed by Batista's army and secret police were students.

What changes, then, has the revolution brought to this generation of Cuban students? How have the university reforms affected the individual student and his quest for a personal identity? How do Cuban and American students compare?

To understand the Cuban students of today we must compare them to the generation that went before. The University of Havana, the oldest and largest university in Cuba, was in the 1950's a prism of Cuba's turbulent political life and a training ground for its leaders. Student activists were waging more than a verbal war on the Batista regime from the campus citadel. Their protest showed that when governments are weak, students can be strong. As in the 1930's when students led the urban resistance to the Machado regime (during which the University was closed for three years), students of the 1950's were actively protesting against a government whose secret police terrorized the city and brought martyrdom, jail, or exile to thousands of students.

Students of the 1950's came to be called the Moncada generation after an abortive attack in 1953 on Batista's Moncada barracks in Oriente, led by Fidel Castro, a recent graduate of the law faculty of the University of Havana. Almost everyone you meet in that generation still in Cuba —now in their 30's and 40's—claims some credit for Batista's downfall, either indirectly, through a martyred brother or exiled friend, or directly, as part of the 26th of July movement, the May 1 movement, or the student-led 13th of March attack on the Presidential palace.

When the Moncada generation—now graduated and part of the establishment—took over, in their green fatigue uniforms, the management of hospitals, stores, farms, and factories, the spirit of top leaders and the paramilitary structure of the Party somehow kept the machinery running despite the fact that political loyalty counted more than training and skill in appointments to key jobs.

To its successors, the Moncada generation appears as a generation of doers and pragmatists—of active Quixotes rather than contemplative Hamlets.

The post-Moncada generation, now 18 to 25 years old, has taken a different role in Cuban history, not as destroyers of the old but as builders of the new. As children they watched and heard the revolution come to power, as adolescents they became its young assistants, and as university students they stepped into a newly reconstructed university. In the literacy campaign of 1961, 45,000 of these teenagers volunteered to live with peasant families for six to eight months, spreading the gospel of the revolution to the countryside and teaching basic literacy. (A is for *agricultura*, R is for *revolución* and so on.) They came to know the peasants for the first time not as passers of arms and food but as students and political converts. Predictably, the campaign taught the predominantly urban middle-class youngsters as much as it taught the peasants. One student recalled, "No one in the family I taught had been to school before; there were no schools close enough to walk or ride by horse to and return within a day . . . I slept in a hammock outside the hut, to avoid the insects. The father taught me how to kill snakes and drain them of oil. We used the oil in the lamp we read by in the evening. . . . I tried to explain to my family that the earth was round, but they insisted that it was flat. They knew the fields were flat." Many lessons were drawn from newspaper articles, and as another student later recounted, "I decided to explain to my family that Gagarin, the Russian astronaut had tried to reach the moon. They wouldn't believe me. I was too young to know. How could a man reach the moon? The moon is a virgin which no man may touch. . . ." The student went on, "I took them on their first trip to Havana. They were afraid to cross the street. They waited for four and a half hours for a bus because they didn't know where to look for the number of the bus."

If the literacy campaign was a cultural crusade against rural feudalism, it was also a training ground in self-sufficiency for its young teachers. It accustomed them to authority, to improvising solutions to unpredictable problems, and it forged a spiritual link to the Moncada generation. Although no student mentioned this, the experience might also have made them less envious of the great comforts of the urban upper class toward which they were oriented. At the same time, it probably made them thankful for the urban comforts they did have, comforts conspicuously absent from peasant life.

The post-Moncada generation, like the generation before it, has lived a period of history which "deprivatized" them by putting a public revolutionary claim on their private lives. Their future does not, as Kenneth Keniston says of alienated American youth, "inspire scant enthusiasm." It is not the dread thing it appeared to be to the soft-faced "graduate" (in the film) standing inert on an automatic conveyor belt in a Los Angeles airport. The airports of Cuba have few enough planes and parts and pilots, let alone conveyor belts for passengers. For Cuban students before and after the revolution, the task at hand—to end a reign of terror and to move from the idea of a virgin moon to the idea of an astronaut—demands a kind of dedication that would appeal to what Erik Erikson calls "the ideological mind" that marks the period of the "identity crisis." The melding of private ambitions into public goals—the impulse to be part of something larger that sends American youth into Freedom Summers, SDS projects, or the Peace

Corps (to put them all in the same bag)—is the same desire that responds to national demands on the young *sabras* of Cuba.

But beyond that, personal identity seems to have for many in both generations of Cuban students a deeper political dimension. The thousand Cubans a week who renounce their citizenship, and the Voice of America from Miami, are constant reminders of an implicit choice. For those who choose to remain, to be Cuban is, to quote a favorite phrase in revolutionary rhetoric, "to be integrated into the revolution." There are strong social pressures to actively participate in national programs, to spend spare time cutting cane or planting coffee. Militia duty for both men and women students is now compulsory. Behind the willingness of students to respond to these pressures is a mood created by events such as the Bay of Pigs invasion, a sense of immediacy about the threat to the Castro regime that wars in foreign places can seldom match. For the main-stream of American youth, the fate of the nation is, by contrast, more remote and the link between self and nation less direct.

Young people in Cuba, more than their American counterparts, are celebrated as a "chosen people." There are plaques and billboards throughout towns and villages bearing the names of young patriotic martyrs of bygone struggles; political rhetoric dates the birth of the country itself to the revolution and a majority of those in positions of power in Cuba are under 30. As Gilda Betancourt, the 25-year-old chairman of the sociology department at the University of Havana, explained, "You have to be young to take all the changes. Last month I went out to cut cane for a month and when I came back, my office had been changed, new programs had been proposed, old plans discarded. It was hard getting back to my old daily pattern. It would be almost impossible if I were 50."

Their ability to act as a shock absorber of change, their

willingness to innovate, to be ideologically committed, make the youth a ready and trusted workforce to replace those whose commitments, if not their training, are outmoded. The complaints of the young are not that they are denied adulthood but that they are hurried into it, that they have "never been young." Indeed they look with some envy at the new, more leisured generation—now 14 to 18 —who conceal skin-tight jeans under their baggy, tan school uniforms.

The situation is otherwise for American youth who are, by contrast, worshipped but not honored. They are supposed to "enjoy the best years of their lives" but remain, like the ladylove of the chivalrous knight, functionless on the pedestal.

While the Moncada and post-Moncada generations share characteristics which distinguish them from American students, the post-Moncada generation differs spiritually if not politically from its predecessor. The post-Moncada generation is critical of the puritanical intolerance of ideological or sexual deviance that characterizes the revolutionary Moncada generation. (Homosexuals are barred from the Party and a talented writer in the Faculty of Letters was discharged from the University for being an open homosexual.) A Moncada fighter, who now sits in an office and assigns scholarships to students, is notorious among students for withholding money from girls known to have slept with their boyfriends. Cuba does not import the pill.

Although this may not be a general difference, my impression is that the younger generation has more of a sense of humor about the revolution and its rhetoric than do their elders. The newspapers, radio, and posters advertise the notion of moral rather than material incentives for work. A young poet described doing productive labor (voluntary agricultural work) one weekend in the company of some older party functionnaires. As they sliced along the rows of sugar cane, he playfully remarked to his neighbor,

"Since the price of sugar is only 2 cents on the world market, why don't we import rather than export sugar? That way we can save money and stop work." The man stared at him blankly, then patiently began to explain why Cuba had to export sugar, much to the young poet's dismay.

Just as a generation of protest gave way to a generation of acceptance, so the university, once a citadel of revolt, is now "integrated into the revolution." The education it offers points students to the task of putting the Economic Plan into effect—off of paper and into goods and services.

The university has been retailored to make useful quasi-generalists of doctors, economists, architects, chemists, engineers, teachers, and dentists—to breed a new model of man for whom academic and vocational life, intellect and action, national, group, and individual loyalties are more integrated.

But the gains were also losses. The revolution which divided the student generations also divided opinion about the university. To faculty and students who wanted a center of humanistic learning, free of government control, the reforms that began in 1959 were a disaster. The concept of a community of scholars dedicated to the search for truth and to training for the liberal professions went out with the revolution when the university lost the fragile autonomy it once had. Four of the largest faculties—medicine, engineering, architecture, and law—collectively refused to accept the authority of the *Federación Estudiantil Universitaria* (which claims that university autonomy was being used for counterrevolutionary ends) and resigned.

Today, a growing minority of students compete for and are selected into the Young Communist organization: Journalism and political science have the highest proportion of members, but 900 of 4,000 students in the technology faculty also belong. The criteria for membership bear on all aspects of life—revolutionary dedication, moral uprightness, and good grades. But once accepted by the Party, the threat of withdrawal can result in repression: One student was "separated" (as opposed to expelled) from the YC because she planned to take up art as well as the more useful vocation of medicine.

On the other hand, those who support the reforms say that the university has put into effect priorities for university resources more in line with the needs of Cuba's underdeveloped economy. Before the revolution the university was out of touch with economic realities. Between 1925 and 1930 the University graduated 2,830 students among whom were only eight electrical engineers, one agricultural engineer, and 12 sugar engineers. Eight hundred and ninety-one students graduated in law.

As Castro asked in a speech, "Do you know how many (students) have been trying to enter the diplomatic service at the University of Havana? Three thousand students. And do you know how many wanted to study economics? Not even one hundred!"

Since 1960 the University of Havana and its two off-spring, the University of Las Villas (4,000 students) and Oriente (5,300 students), have become vocational training centers. Its former three faculties (law, medicine, and letters and arts) have grown to eight: technology, agronomy, medicine, sciences, teaching, economy, humanities, and the workers and peasant faculty—an adult extension division which prepares its 4,000 lower-class students to enter one of the other seven faculties, usually technology or agriculture. The most important of these and the largest is the 30-million-dollar new Faculty of Technology (the *Ciudad Universitaria*), which enrolls 4,000 students, over half of whom are on complete scholarships.

For all students, textbooks are free at any bookstore, many of which are stocked with medical and technical tomes written in English and printed offset by the Cuban Book Institute, in defiance of international copyright laws.

The experiment with priorities has put every field of learning into a state of constant flux. One recent graduate in arts from the University of Oriente complained, "The first year they told us that we would learn linguistics when we specialize, after we got a foundation. The second year they told us that linguistics *was* the foundation." Students having to repeat a second-year course found that it was not the *same* second-year course that they had previously flunked.

According to the vice-rector of the University of Havana, "The university is not designed to develop specialists. It is designed to develop useful people." (After a two-hour interview, the vice-rector, who was also a professor of medicine and a practicing doctor, excused himself because he had to perform an operation.) These changes toward pragmatism have meant that technology students become people who can run factories, not researchers. For doctors, it means more who can vaccinate children, fewer who can transplant organs. For economists, it means more general consultants and planners and fewer specialists in particular fields (and no private businessmen). This does not mean the elimination of specialization, but a reduction of it, as the needs of rural areas are met.

Pure research, though minimal, is not absent from the new priorities, and all research has been turned over to the National Center of Scientific Research and the Academy of Sciences. Professors are promoted by student-faculty committees on the basis of ability to teach and "revolutionary commitment," rather than on research.

Like small American colleges, there is little social distance between teacher and student. In some cases the same person is formally both. The mass exodus of professors at the time of the revolution and again in 1960 left the university bereft of its most precious resource. According to the vice-rector of the University, all but 13 of some 300 medical professors left, and that was typical of other faculties. As a stopgap measure, recent graduates and top students in their last years have been appointed to the faculty. Sixty percent of the faculty of technology in 1968 were either recent graduates or undergraduates in their fourth or fifth year. The psychology department had four faculty members with the equivalent of a Ph.D., and the chemistry department had one. A Cuban report to UNESCO showed "teaching personnel" at the University of Havana as 2,222 in the beginning of 1965 and 3,017 in the beginning of 1966; most of the additions were students.

If the lines of authority within the university are blurred, it is partly because professors and students see each other in so many different contexts. Almost every field of training—called a *carrera*—has a program of "preprofessional work" that sends professor and student out into the field together, for anywhere from two weeks to two months a year.

"Preprofessional work" orients the student toward a vocation, and gives him a basis for "relevance" in his academic studies, just as the correspondence courses after graduation suggest the relevance of academic studies to his vocation. Like the system of "productive labor" (voluntary agricultural or factory work), it shows him what needs to be done, and gives him some idea of where he could do his two years of social service, which are now compulsory for all university graduates.

The blend of classroom and field work is different for each university, each faculty, and each school. But in one way or another, each school divides its students into small groups called *equipos,* which work together in the countryside at something deemed educative and also economically (and in some cases politically) useful. Last year students in construction engineering joined a team of engineers who were building roads in Camaguey Province. An *equipo* of chemical engineers worked in a fertilizer factory, talking to workers and analyzing the products at various stages of production. Medical students vaccinated sugar-cane cutters, and dentistry students examined the teeth of peasants. Students in geography analyzed soils of different regions. Law students participated in "people's courts" in the Isle of Pines.

One *equipo* of about 33 economics students devised new production methods in a grapefruit juice factory in the Isle of Pines and wrote a report both for their university requirement and for the National Institute of Agrarian Reform, the introduction and conclusion of which was required reading for all other economics students. (Calculations were made on the university computer.) At the same time the office staff in the factory had a hand in the report and was taught how to plan by the economics students. The students, who in their first, second, and third year had read Keynes and Samuelson as well as Marx, were arguing about the applications of Frederick Taylor to the division of labor in the grapefruit juice factory, and had concluded that too much division of labor would harm worker morale. Their plan called for rotating workers—so that everyone could have a hand at all the kinds of work (mostly semiskilled)—and for monthly meetings to "orient" (which has the connotation of "explain" or "tell") the workers about the relation of little tasks to the whole plan.

Half of the 62 students in their third year of journalism do their preprofessional training by running *El Mundo,* one of Havana's two metropolitan daily newspapers. Its editor, a 27-year-old newspaperman, said that "graduates will go to provincial newspapers, though some may want to send an article or two from the field. They like it. Last year they visited newspapers and did a study of how people read a newspaper, but they like running the paper better. They learn more."

In the afternoon and evening, some of the five part-time teachers supervise students who make up various sections of the newspapers. In the morning, classes are held in the office and the faults in yesterday's front page are inspected and discussed. The conflict between the demands of training journalists, which requires rotation of personnel, and the demands of getting the paper to press on time has resulted in a series of snags. A student may be just getting the feel of the European news section when he is switched to sports, which he knows little about. There is also the problem of staggering student vacations so that enough students will be continually working on the paper. One journalism student commented, "It was chaos at first. But we know that we have a lot of readers and we have to learn fast. It's exciting, I didn't know whether I wanted to be a journalist before when we just visited newspapers; running one has helped me decide to be a journalist."

For this journalism student, the irrelevance of his education was not a complaint. And for most university students a vocation was something they practiced more than wondered about.

Preprofessional work in all fields integrates the postrevolution generation of students into the economic experiments of their elders, an experience which both the Moncada generation in Cuba and American students could only privately improvise, or for various reasons would resist. The educational system seems to curb the growth of political or hippie or collegiate subcultures within the university walls and to discourage the nonstudent fringe by the educational hurdles between them and an interesting job. Just as people living under food rations learn the virtue of thrift, so students who balk at the"irrelevance" of their education are considered a luxury the revolution cannot afford.

While the relevance of education is not an issue to this generation of Cuban students, they do object to being railroaded into careers that are of little interest to them but are of high priority to the state. Most agree that the needs of the revolution ought to be filled within the parameters of one's own personal needs, interests, and talents, except in times of political crisis—although sometimes students disagree about what constitutes a crisis and whether Cuba is in one now.

According to Paul Goodman, a youth seeks his identity in the "nether-netherland" between what he likes to do, what he is good at, and what needs doing. If what needs doing is determined in a capitalist country by the market, it is determined in a socialist country such as Cuba by the Economic Plan.

The notion of "the integrated man" which underlies higher education in Cuba is also behind the program of voluntary "productive labor," which sends students to one of the University's 11 farms for a weekend a month and one month in the summer.

I worked on one University farm in the cordon, or greenbelt, which circles Havana, in which 70 or so of the 280 students in Letters from the humanities faculty collectively do their stint. An ambitious six-year plan had designated the land, formerly a hog farm, to be converted into a botanical garden harboring every major species of plant in the tropical world. Greatly lacking the latest technology, the men students used an ox to draw their cart when the tractor broke down—which it often did—and the women were planting little pieces of grass in tin cans to make a mall which might have been more efficiently done with lawn seed had that been available.

In addition to the students there were 20 professors and the janitor from the University, all of whom worked and lived together in the men's or women's barracks on the farm. Paid day laborers and a group of prospective emigrants, who must work for at least three months in order to leave the country, worked on the farm and commuted home to Havana in the evening. Work began at 7:00 and continued until 5:00 at a steady if not arduous pace, with a short break at 10:00 and the traditional two-hour lunch and siesta break.

As they bent over the cans, with the sound of rifle practice in the distance, students sang nursery rhymes in Latin
—there was a favorite Latin teacher in the group—and
American pop songs including "San Francisco," "My Little
Darling," from the 1950's, and all the Beatles' songs. They
regaled each other with anti-Chinese jokes and discussed
divorced friends; there have been many divorces since the
revolution. They talked about the housing shortage in Havana; some married couples lived with their parents while
waiting for their name to come up on the university housing list. They occasionally played a "guess who I'm thinking about" game where yes and no answers led the group
to a name someone had in mind; the name was often that
of an American movie star who played in movies ten years
ago (no American films have been shown in Cuba since
the embargo on American goods), although one Russian
professor who had studied six years in the Soviet Union
always named Soviet artists and scientists unknown to the
group. No Chinese name came up while I was there.

Finally in the evening after work, groups of students
huddled in circles outside the barracks around a tiny kero-
sene heater that held a tiny pot of precious, rationed coffee
brought from various homes. The tin cup of coffee went
ceremoniously around the circle until it was gone, and the
students argued about the Bolivian minister of Interior who
had given Che Guevera's diary to Castro. They sang
Beatles' songs and sentimental Spanish songs in an exaggerated warble on into the night.

Living together and sharing common deprivations, tasks,
and aims resulted in a natural communal spirit. They didn't
talk about or contrive community; with all its advantages
and disadvantages, they had it.

The post-Moncada generation tend to be culturally oriented toward the North, politically to the South. They tend
to talk of coffee rather than community, of integration into
the revolution rather than cooptation by it, of the practi-

calities of their vocation, rather than "irrelevance" of what they learn, of political loyalty and technical knowhow, rather than of College Board scores and Graduate Record exams, of the needs of the revolution rather than personal ambitions, of a teacher's good and bad points rather than his remoteness, and of responsibilities rather than—in spite of the legacy—protest.

The third generation of Cuban youth, now in their teens, as the benefactor of the revolution, has what the post-Moncada generation in grandfatherly tones call a "safe, comfortable life." They are given free schooling, free meals, board, and books. The revolutionary heroism is someone else's story, a source of vicarious pride. Their battle is the more mundane one of loosening parental constraints and shaping a life in which miniskirts or long hair are not a revolutionary sin. It is hard to know how many high-school students are trying to be ordinary teenagers, but the second generation goes along with school measures that remind the young of the hard life, the debt. The post-Moncada generation echoes the Party's hope that the toughness and youth of the country will become its permanent feature, that each generation will, as the saying goes, "give the flag" to the next, but countries, like individuals, do not remain young: The flag changes meaning, and what it is to be young changes with history.

Cuban youth, like Cuba itself, should rightfully be compared to the pre-revolutionary generation in Cuba or to present Bolivian, Chilean, or Israeli youth, not to American or French youth. But there is some use in comparing them to the youth of postindustrial countries such as the United States because of the light it sheds on American students and their search for personal identity. Different societies put different burdens on the answers to the questions: "who am I, what shall I be, what shall I do?" American youth are less integrated into the social and political life of their country, and life is less harsh than in Cuba. They are socially kept young longer and get older without becoming adult. The country itself is taking only what might be called an "identity check-up." Cuban youth, by contrast, are if anything *too* integrated into the social, economic, and political life of their country. They are given adulthood without demanding it. They can readily identify with the generation of young heroes, Che, its martyred saint and Fidel, its St. Peter, that went before and now hold power, a generation which has improvised an educational system that beckons them, honors them, pays for them, mobilizes them, and rewards them with positions of responsibility and authority. It also politicizes them, militarizes them, and restricts them as the family and Church did before.

Consequently, what sense of indecision does characterize Cuban adolescents does not in itself distinguish them from their elders in power. If in any society it is a minority who experience an identity crisis, in Cuba the minority is smaller. The term *identity crisis* is as inflated when applied to Cuban youth as the term *revolution* is when applied to American universities. The identity crisis, itself born of the "psychosocial moratorium on adulthood" is like the hippie movement, another luxury of a complex and affluent society which a revolution in earnest does without.

April 1969

POSTSCRIPT:

This article is not based on a systematic survey but on a series of in-depth interviews with students, faculty and administrators of the University of Havana. Besides Jose Yglesias' "Cuba Report: Their Hippies, Their Squares" (The New York Times Magazine, January 12, 1968) and Wassily Leontief's "Notes on a Visit to Cuba," (The New York Review of Books, August 21, 1969) there have been no published articles on Cuban student life in the late sixties. The experimental nature of Cuban social engineering makes writing about it risky. Descriptions of particular projects are as quickly outdated as the projects themselves. For example, the project of training journalists at El Mundo, one of Havana's two major newspapers, was stopped in

1969 when the newspaper itself folded due to the paper shortage.

Note on University Life:

For a description of university life before the revolution see Andres Suarez, *Cuba: Castroism and Communism 1959-1966*, (Cambridge: MIT Press, 1967). As Suarez points out, the students who returned from prison or exile after Machado's downfall in 1933 took virtual control of the university, with the good wishes of the "revolutionary" government then in power, thus setting a partial precedent for the events of the sixties. Ironically, an American Foreign Policy Commission, writing in 1935, noted that the majority of university students "were older by three years than subsequent student groups will be, and matured by the responsibilities and activities of three years of revolution, an experience through which no other generation of students should have to pass." *Problems of the New Cuba: Report of the Commission on Cuban Affairs* (New York: Foreign Policy Association, Inc., 1935, p. 154).

The university under the impact of the revolution is described by Luis Boza Dominquez, an émigré professor, in *La Situacion Universitaria en Cuba* (Editorial Del Pacifico, 1962). It is also touched on in Theodore Draper's *Castro's Revolution: Myths and Realities* (New York: Praeger, 1962, esp. p. 14). Also see Enrique Gonzales Pedrere, *La Revolucion Cubana*, (Mexico: Universidad Nacional Autonomía de Mexico, 1959); Pedro Vicente Aja, "La Crisis de la Universidad de La Habana," *Guadernos*, no. 47, March-April 1961, pp. 18-25; Carlos Rafael Rodriquez, "La Reforma Universitaria," in *Cuba Socialista*, February, 1962, pp. 22-44, which portrays the university reforms as an offshoot of the "Moviemento de Cordoba" in Argentina in 1918. For the impact of political events on generations see Maurice Zeitlin, *Revolutionary Politics and the Cuban Working Class*, chapter 9, "Political Generations" (Princeton, New Jersey: Princeton University Press, 1967) and Karl Mannheim, *Essays on the Sociology of Knowledge*, chapter 7, "The Problem of Generations" (Paul Keckskemeti, editor, New York: Oxford University Press, 1952). Orthodox Marxists in Cuba do not concede any conflict other than class conflict, but the issue of generational conflict among Cuban intellectuals was publicly debated in *La Gaceta de Cuba* (April-May 1966).

Note on Political Organization:

Few sources deal with political organization in the university since the revolution. In 1955 there were 26 communists (seven cells) in the university (See Suarez, ibid, p. 7). In 1968, according to the general secretary of the Young Communists in the Faculty of Technology, there were 900 party members out of 4000 students. Each July 26th, students nominated for Vanguardia are voted on by the entire student body. Vanguardia members are eligible to join the Young Communists; every year from 50 to 150 Vanguardia members join the ranks of the Young Communists.

Note on the "New Man":

One of the aims of the Party is to create "the New Man" who responds to moral and not material incentives, who enjoys his work and who puts the claims of the revolution above private ambition. More precisely, the new man does not put the claims of the revolution *above* private ambition; his private ambition is not at odds with his social obligations and he wants to do what he has to do.

The academic version of the "New Man" is being trained by the C.N.I.C., set up in 1964. The 200 graduate students now in training will teach later in the university and, according to the vice-rector of the University of Havana, the policy is to avoid a narrow scientific orientation, and to develop generalists and well-rounded people. E. N. Eisenstadt notes the stress, among Israeli youth, on a well-rounded personality, not limited by occupational blinders. (*From Generation to Generation,* New York: Free Press, 1956, p. 236.) While the image of the "New Man" serves, as Eisenstadt points out, to accentuate the differences between the generations, Cubans are trying to change the old men too. Of course many of the older generation have left Cuba. (At the time of the revolution, those faculty members who left the university were Cuban since the law at that time forbade employing foreign professors. Today there are about a hundred foreign professors, mainly in technological fields.)

Note on Attitude toward American Youth:

Cuban students are generally intrigued with the hippie subculture in the United States. They associate it with drugs (which went out with the revolution) and Beatles music. (A Beatles record underarm is a status symbol. They somehow manage to erase music from records imported before 1958 and re-record Beatles music.) However, they also consider the hippie movement a bourgeois perversion of the image of the "New Man" and see the hippies as the "children of the empire at play." The interest in, but lack of identification with hippies, is no accident; despite the primitive communism of some hippie groups, the present generation of Cubans could not be more different. It is as integrated into its society, as oriented toward the future and vocational life, as hard working, thrifty and extroverted as the hippies are opposed to their society, present-oriented, leisured and introspective.

For example, the hippie interest in astrology only amuses or bewilders the Cuban revolutionary whose task is to uproot traditional "superstition" among the peasantry. Differences between the two groups extend even to the *modes* of ego diffusion which, according to Erikson, characterize the unsuccessful quest for identity. If hippies or hippie-sympathizers sometimes deny or avoid the question of identity through passive observation of their "inner forces," Cuban revolutionaries seem to dismiss the same question by an acquiescence, equally passive, to the outer dictates of the economic plan.

The Revolutionary Offensive

CARMELO MESA-LAGO

On March 13, 1968, almost ten years after his revolution, Fidel Castro launched a "revolutionary offensive" in Cuba. This campaign is a crucial step on the Cuban path toward the construction of a socialist society and represents an acceleration of an economic policy emphasizing capital accumulation and rapid development even at the cost of less consumption.

Goals and Tools

According to the newspaper of the Cuban Communist Party (P.C.C.), the revolutionary offensive intends to fight selfishness and individualism and to eradicate parasitism. To this end the government confiscated 55,636 small, private businesses. Some 31 percent of these were retail food outlets—corner groceries, butcher shops, poultry and fish stores, and vegetable and fruit stands. Another 26 percent provided consumer services—laundries, dry cleaners, barber shops, photo shops, lodging and boarding houses, and shoe and auto repair shops. Such food and drink businesses as bars, restaurants, and snack shops represented another 21 percent. Finally, 17 percent sold garments, shoes, hats, furniture, cigarettes, books, flowers, hardware, and electrical appliances; and the rest (5 percent) were small handicrafts manufacturing plastic, leather, rubber, wood, metal, and chemical products, and textiles, perfumes, and tobacco.

Castro said that these private businesses, embracing almost one third of consumer goods distribution, were growing rapidly and making more and more profits. The fact is that the private sector has been filling the vacuum created by the inefficient operation of state services. Half of the entrepreneurs did not have employees in their businesses, but the other half hired people at higher wages than those paid by the state.

Some 20,000 owners had worked as wage earners before they started their own businesses. Most had established them after the revolution in 1959. The Party newspaper strongly criticized them: "It is intolerable that a worker, whose labor may benefit the whole people, should become a potential bourgeois, a self-centered money grabber and exploiter of his countrymen."

One-third of the enterprises have now been closed. For the rest, new managers, most of them housewives, were selected from the Committees for the Defense of the Revolution (C.D.R.)—a state organization principally engaged in hunting counterrevolutionaries. The former owners had two alternatives: to continue as employees in their own shops or to work on the state farms or on the roads. Towards the end of May, 1968, the Ministry of Labor reported that out of 36,506 former entrepreneurs who had received medical checkups 16,671 were physically able persons, 85 percent of them already working in state jobs. In addition, an increasing number of self-employed workers are being rapidly incorporated into the state sector.

The only private activity left is agriculture, where 150,-000 small farmers still own 30 percent of the arable land, all in farms less than 165 acres. They too are supervised by and included in the nationwide plans of development. Members of the Association of Private Farmers (A.N.A.P.) may obtain seed, fertilizer, credit, and other aid from the state. In return, they must sell part of their crop to the state procurement agency (*Acopio*) at a government price set below the market price.

The Collectivization Process in Cuba: 1962, 1964, and 1968 (In percentages)			Table 1
Sectors of the Economy	Percentage Collectivized		
	1962	1964	1968
Agriculture	37	70	70
Industry	85	95	100
Construction	80	98	100
Transportation	92	95	100
Retail trade	52	75	100
Wholesale and foreign trade	100	100	100
Banking	100	100	100
Education	100	100	100

Cuban agricultural cooperatives (similar to Russian *kolkhozy*) where transformed into state farms (similar to *sovkhozy*) by mid-1962. At the beginning, a small plot of land for private cultivation was allowed for the state farm workers, but in 1967 this right was abolished, apparently because workers devoted more time to their plot than to the state land. Therefore, Cuba has a higher degree of land collectivization than most socialist countries. (Within the socialist bloc most land is in *kolkhozy*, except for Poland and Yugoslavia, where private farms are still in the majority.) Now that so many trade and service enterprises have also been nationalized and self-employed workers are moving into the state sector, the P.C.C. has proclaimed: "Cuba has thus become the socialist country with the highest percentage of state-owned property." In less than a decade, the state has appropriated about 90 percent of all production and distribution, plus services.

The future of private agriculture too is uncertain. In November, regional meetings of A.N.A.P. provinces decided upon the total eradication of free-market sales, all agricultural and livestock production to go to the *Acopio*. Dairy farmers in Havana province were being integrated into the state sector. The ostensible reason was their poor productivity (partly caused by the low prices paid by the procurement agency). This resulted in less agricultural products (particularly milk) purchased by the *Acopio*. The government began to buy cows and to pay wages to the farmers.

According to Prime Minister Castro, small farmers used very primitive methods, and this caused low productivity and poor and unstable output. At first, state procurement quotas and prices had tried to cope with the problem, but had failed, mainly because the farmers had the right to sell any product in excess of the *Acopio,* at any price. Castro stated: "We have changed the old system of relations with the farmers . . . because everything that they produce must be either consumed or exported by the country [as a whole]." Now the state is doing all investing in planting, fertilizing, building, and providing technical aid. In turn, the whole harvest is "withdrawn from mercantile distribution"—that is, bought by the state. More than 90 percent of the farmers in a circle of land surrounding Havana have joined the plan, and this is considered a model.

In March 1968, A.N.A.P. said of the merchants: "Driven by their desire for profit making, many of these elements have constantly carried on illegal trade with the farmers, thus preventing the sale of many products to the State Procurement Agency for distribution to the people." In April, A.N.A.P. decided to sell all private production to the state. Since the beginning of the Offensive, "brigades of collective work" and "groups of mutual aid" are being organized among private farms.

Another goal of the offensive is a huge mobilization for higher production, particularly in agriculture, and better ideological control. On one hand, the state is exhorting workers to increase productivity, donate more unpaid work, reinforce labor discipline, and save more. The Party has stressed the necessity of controlling the masses to support the offensive and reject "sectarianism." In Oriente, the campaign headquarters has reported that people are being prepared for a "war economy" and "troops of workers" are being organized and sent to the "production front."

The Confederation of Cuban Workers (C.T.C.) has appealed to the labor force to fulfill tasks with "spirit of sacrifice," "revolutionary heroism," and "harsh will," while suppressing "weaknesses and complaints." In April, 250,-000 unpaid workers were recruited by the C.T.C. to work in agriculture for three or four weeks, 12 hours per day. Some 2.5 million man-days of work were "donated" by unpaid workers who spent 14 weeks on coffee plantations. More than 100 labor brigades are constructing roads and highways. The C.D.R. members have sworn to increase vigilance, recruit more unpaid workers for agriculture, obtain more blood donations, exert pressure upon the people to read official publications, and organize meetings to get the masses to support the Offensive. The Young Communist League (U.J.C.) is committed to recruit 10,000 youngsters in the cities (who will join 40,000 already in service) to work for three years in the fields of the Isle of Pines, now renamed "The Isle of Youth." The Federation of Cuban Women (F.M.C.) is mobilizing its members for the elimination of criticism and rumors against the revolutionary laws and measures. Housewives are asked to watch neighbors, work in agriculture, watch the influence that teachers, "young pioneer" leaders, and playmates exert upon their children, and to educate them in the spirit of Che Guevara.

The offensive also hopes to increase capital accumulation. Castro announced that in 1968 gross investment will equal 31 percent of G.N.P. If this target is fulfilled, the rate of growth over 1967 would be an impressive 87 percent. Table 2 illustrates the increase of investment and G.N.P. in recent years.

The Growth of G.N.P. and Investment in Cuba: 1962-1968 (In millions of *pesos* at current prices)			Table 2
Year	G.N.P.[a]	Gross Investment[b]	I/G.N.P.[c]
1962	3,079	607.6	19.7
1963	3,788	716.8	18.9
1964	4,202	794.9	18.9
1965	4,136	827.1	20.0
1966	4,039	909.8	22.5
1967	n.a.	979.0	n.a.
1968	4,000	1,240.0[d]	31.0[d]

[a] Gross material product. Because it excludes services, actual G.N.P. should be higher; but on the other hand, due to inflation, there is also an upward bias in the figures.
[b] Gross domestic formation of capital.
[c] Percentage of G.N.P. devoted to gross domestic formation of capital.
[d] Official targets; should be taken as indicative only.

These figures must be treated with caution. On one hand, because some relate to gross material product, in the Marxist sense, they exclude the value of services not directly used in production, and therefore actual G.N.P. should be higher. On the other hand, increasing inflation has created an upward-bias tendency in G.N.P. figures since 1960. Price indices have not been published in Cuba since 1959 and G.N.P. figures in Table 2 are given at current prices. Last but not least is the serious problem of reliability of Cuban G.N.P. statistics. All these difficulties indicate that data in Table 2, particularly those for 1968 (official targets) should be taken only as rough indicators.

The Cuban revolutionary offensive is neither new nor isolated, but is the acceleration of a process initiated when the Cuban leadership aligned with "orthodox" Marxism-Leninism. There are two different economic lines within the socialist bloc. The "reformist, pragmatic, or liberal" line was initiated by Yugoslavia, and after Stalin's death, spread throughout East Europe reaching the U.S.S.R. in the 1960's. Features of this line are the tendency toward economic and administrative decentralization: price reform; increasing autonomy granted to managers concerning enterprise profits; more use of economic incentives and market mechanisms; and in some countries, revival of private initiative in agriculture, trade, tourism, and handicrafts.

The other line of thought, led by China, is more "orthodox, doctrinaire, or conservative." (The use of such labels may be very confusing, since each side accuses the other of "rightist" tendencies.) Outstanding characteristics of this line are highly centralized economy and planning system;

Agricultural Production in Cuba: 1957-1966 (Index Numbers: 1952-56 = 100)									Table 3
	1957-58	58-59	59-60	60-61	61-62	62-63	63-64	64-65	65-66
Total Production	113	114	117	133	106	94	100	122	101
Per Capita Production	106	104	105	117	92	80	83	99	80

trend toward the nationalization of all means of production; nonmaterial or "moral" incentives (such as revolutionary enthusiasm, socialist emulation, granting of medals, banners, pennants, and diplomas); political education to eliminate selfish inclinations and develop a "new man"; and financing of enterprises through the state budget (that is, most enterprise profits are taxed away by the state, which follows its own criteria for investment, disregarding profitability). Cuba belongs to this group, although its quarrels with China clearly indicate its independence.

As private enterprise and economic incentives have been replaced by state enterprise, central planning, and moral stimuli, agricultural production has gradually declined. The fall in output is mainly the result of the ill-fated "anti-sugar" policy enforced by the government in 1959-63, together with errors in state planning; but it was also caused by the elimination of material incentives that induced a diminution in labor efforts and in management concern for enterprise efficiency. Data from the United Nations shows that agricultural output rose in the period 1958-61 when most of the land was still privately owned, but declined sharply afterwards with the exception of 1964-65. In 1965-66 total agricultural production was 32 percent below the 1960-61 level. The decline was even worse per capita. In 1961 sugar almost reached the prerevolutionary record (7 million tons in 1952). The 1962-64 crops were among the lowest in the precedent 15 years, and in 1965-68 there have been good and bad crops in alternating years. The Long-Term Sugar Plan for 1965-70 has been fulfilled in the first year only. Nonfulfillment in 1966-68 has ranged from 19 to 38 percent.

For nonsugar crops, the United Nations Economic Commission for Latin America (E.C.L.A.) has reported that between 1960 and 1966 there was a decline in cereals (33 percent), tubers and starchy roots (6 percent), pulses (6 percent), oil seeds (64 percent), nonalcoholic beverages (20 percent), fibers (34 percent), and other crops (12 percent). Fruit output was stagnant. Livestock production between 1961 and 1966 declined 6 percent; in per capita figures, 12 percent.

Mining, the third most important line of Cuba's production has also been declining. Practically all mineral extraction including nickel, copper, manganese, iron ore and crude oil, had decreased between 1957-58 and 1965. Only in salt was there a substantial increase in output.

The decline in sugar, agricultural, and mining output has hurt Cuban foreign trade. Having less to export (sugar still makes up from 80 to 85 percent) and having larger imports, the national debt has been growing steadily, especially after collectivization was accelerated in 1960-61.

Cuban Foreign Trade: 1957-1966 (In millions of *pesos*)				Table 4
Years	Exports[a] f.o.b.	Imports[b] c.i.f.	Transactions	Balance
1957	807.7	772.9	1,580.6	+ 34.8
1958	733.5	771.1	1,510.6	− 37.6
1959	637.7	742.2	1,380.0	−104.5
1960	618.2	637.9	1,256.1	− 19.7
1961	624.9	702.6	1,327.5	− 77.7
1962	520.6	759.2	1,279.8	−238.6
1963	542.9	866.2	1,409.1	−323.3
1964	713.8	1,008.5	1,722.3	−294.7
1965	686.0	865.0	1,551.0	−179.0
1966	592.0	926.0	1,518.0	−334.0

Cumulative balance of trade
1951-1958 = + 420.0
1959-1966 = −1,571.5

[a] Exports f.o.b. = excluding cost of shipping.
[b] Exports c.i.f. = including cost of shipping and insurance.

As documented in Table 4, in 1957 there was a positive balance of trade of 34.8 million pesos, while in 1966 the balance was negative by 334 million pesos. A cumulative balance of trade for 1959-66 shows a trade deficit greater than 1.5 billion pesos. The U.S.S.R. has provided generous loans to offset the imbalance, but this has added the problem of repayment—which deteriorates the situation even further. Official figures indicate that the proportion of the state budget devoted to "repayment of the national debt" and "reserve" grew from 7.4 percent in 1963 to 18.8 percent in 1965. At the same time, all other categories of the budget went down, particularly that of investments in the economy, which declined from 41.6 percent in 1963 to 34.4 percent in 1965.

But despite all this—and despite the fact that most socialist countries have been increasing material incentives and decreasing centralized control—Cuba has become more and more uncompromising toward private initiative and material rewards. Castro calls this "true Marxism-Leninism" and told Herbert L. Matthews in late 1967 that "Communist countries like Russia are becoming more capitalistic because they are relying on material incentives more and more."

On July 26, 1968, Castro gave his blueprint for the future. Material incentive will be phased out and replaced by moral ones; the connection between work for and wages from an enterprise will be broken, and citizens will develop a relationship between their effort on behalf of the society and the free goods and services directly granted by the state. (The government already supplies free education, medical care, social security, burials, telephone calls, nurseries—and, for some, recreation and housing.) In the future, all housing, meals, clothing, transportation, communication, public utilities, and entertainment will be free. Income differences will be gradually abolished and distribution made according to needs. Hence, there will be no social classes. In the future Cuban society, an engineer will earn as much as a cane cutter.

By mid-1968, Cuba had become the leader of the "orthodox" line within the socialist world, while Czechoslovakia was rapidly passing Yugoslavia in liberalization. Castro's support of the Soviet invasion of Czechoslovakia should therefore be explained in this light.

Cuba is not the first socialist country that tried to build communism on moral stimuli. The U.S.S.R. briefly took this path under Trotsky's influence, following the Bolshevik Revolution in 1917. But this experiment, together with the devastation caused by the civil war, ended in a grave economic crisis; and Lenin had to "go back two steps" and launch the "New Economic Policy" (N.E.P.), based on the partial reestablishment of private ownership and material rewards. Once the Soviet economy was reconstructed, Stalin could push collectivization again; but he did not reject material stimuli altogether. When in early 1960 the Soviet economy showed signs of decay, Soviet leaders—now supported by Yevsei Liberman's theories—stressed material incentives more.

The "Great Leap Forward" by China in 1958-59 marks the most grandiose attempt of socialist country to use moral incentives on a large scale. The keystone was the system of communes, with the principal feature the distribution of the collective product according to communal needs, instead of individual work. But it ended in the economic depression of 1960-61 and the restoration of material incentives. According to Western specialists, the failure cost China a decade of growth. In 1965-67, Mao Tse-tung and Lin Piao led a new campaign: "The Great Proletarian Cultural Revolution." Apparently it too has been called off because of fears of another crisis.

The Cuban government, on three prior occasions in 1964, had sought the advice of the French Marxist agronomist René Dumont. The internationally known specialist criticized the acceleration of socialization and reminded the Cubans of what happened in the U.S.S.R. in 1918-21. He also warned them against the highly centralized system of planning and administration, the nationalization of small enterprises, the elimination of agricultural cooperatives (*kolkhozy*), the gigantic size of state farms, the lack of financial autonomy of enterprises, and the disdain for material incentives. He was categorical: ". . . to trust in moral stimuli as substitutes for material rewards will lead to the reinitiation—in a voluntarily and unuseful way—of the cycle of errors perpetrated by other socialist countries . . . disregard the high price already paid by such mistakes." But the Cuban leaders have ignored all warnings.

Economic problems as well as political difficulties, both of internal and international scope, have made the offensive necessary. As Cuba has become more radical ideologically, the difficulties with the U.S.S.R have increased. In

1968 Castro complained that the Soviets had rejected the request for more oil and that the shortage could slow Cuba's economic development.

Three weeks later he accused a few Party members, who followed the Soviet line, of a conspiracy. The apparent leader of this "microfaction" was Aníbal Escalante, who in 1962 had fled to Czechoslovakia after a dispute with Castro. Other officials involved were José Matar, former national coordinator of the C.D.R., and Ramón Calcines, director of the state enterprise in charge of fruit production, both of the Central Committee of the P.C.C. These three and eight other Party members were found guilty of: "Attacks by means of intrigue, on the principal measures of the revolution; distribution of clandestine propaganda against line of the Party; presenting of false, calumnious data about the plans of the revolution to officials of foreign countries; taking of secret documents from the Central Committee and the Ministry of Basic Industry; and proselytizing and furthering of ideological divergences. . . ." They were kicked out of the party.

On February 3, 1968, Escalante was condemned to 15 years in prison by the Revolutionary Court, the ten Party members received 12 years, and another 26 people got from two to 10 years.

Actually, the trial was an accusation that the Soviet Union had intervened in Cuban internal affairs. One Soviet embassy official, Rudolf Shliapnikov, was linked with them. A resolution of the Political Board of the P.C.C. not to send a delegation to the meeting of Communist Parties at Budapest, as well as approving a drastic plan to save fuel, was publicized alongside the sanctions against the "microfaction." During the trial, it was claimed that the illegal acts of the "microfaction" had climaxed in July 1967; but Castro waited six months before making his accusation. This was the most propitious moment, precisely when he acknowledged the difficulties in the Soviet supply of oil.

(Another reason for the trial could have been the failure of Guevara in Bolivia.) Announcing the Offensive in March 1968, the Prime Minister referred to the "microfaction" as a group supporting "reformist and reactionary policies." He also said: ". . . not all problems can be dealt with publicly . . . because there are questions of diplomatic nature that could be harmful if they were known by the enemy."

It is obvious that the offensive includes a clever stratagem to reinforce Castroite autonomy vis-a-vis Moscow. But this does not mean that Cuba is willing to yield ideologically—quite the contrary: "Some have said that it would be good to see a type of tropical Titoism implemented here. What an absurd idea, what a ridiculous idea, to believe that the revolution could conceivably regress to rightist positions. . . . What we are going to have here is communism and more communism, real communism!"

The offensive is also Castro's new blow against stabilizing the revolution. His desire for power and the personality cult he fosters are serious barriers to administrative decentralization, the enactment of a "socialist" political Constitution, and the granting of more decision-making power to the lower echelons in the administration. Castro is Prime Minister of the government, First Secretary of the Party, Commander in Chief of the Armed Forces, President of the Central Planning Board, and Director of I.N.R.A.—truly the "maximum" leader. Further, the elimination of Soviet support and the death of Guevara—the former leader of the Peking line—have left Castro as sole ideologist and guide of the revolution.

The offensive has brought eulogies from "orthodox" socialist countries like North Korea, but criticism from *Pravda*. A Hungarian newspaper suggested that Escalante and the others had really been condemned for their criticism of Castro's one-man leadership, the decreasing influence of the trade unions, and the irregularity of Central Committee meetings. On May Day, Raúl Castro, Minister of the Armed Forces, referred to this criticism of the "non-capitalist press": ". . . some have said that we are idealists, romantics, and adventurers, that we are violating the laws of economics, that we have decided to reach our goals by substituting enthusiasm for economic principles." He added: "To say that the small merchants lived better because they were influenced by material incentives is true. And for that very reason, we reject material incentives. We don't want a small-merchant mentality for our people!"

The fact is, however, that less ideological reasons—like the shortage of consumer goods—may be the real causes for rejecting economic incentives. Castro has asked: "Are we going to encourage the people by offering them more money with which they could buy nothing?"

Production troubles have been significant as causes for starting the Offensive. Sugar output for 1968 was about 35 percent short of target, and this casts a deep shadow on the 1970 goal of 10 million tons, which would require a 100 percent increase in two years. But to Castro this goal has become a test of the revolution, and a mobilization of all available human and material resources is taking place to achieve it. Castro has accused the "microfaction"—and hence the U.S.S.R.—of assuring the failure of the sugar plan, thereby forcing Cuban leaders to become "more calm, more docile, more submissive."

Consumer goods difficulties have also caused trouble. Between January 1967 and January 1968 state purchases fell by 14 percent. Purchases of eggs, rice, edible oils, meat, and beans were stagnant—which actually meant a decline per capita. Adults no longer have a milk quota. This measure, together with gasoline rationing, resulted in hoarding and long queues in front of state stores. The Prime Minister claimed that supply difficulties have caused "protests, discontent, confusion, and dissatisfaction" because the people still had not shed "ideological weaknesses," "bourgeois customs," and lack of "day-to-day heroism." To correct this situation, a systematic, ideological campaign is being developed through all communication media and by state bodies that aim to control the youth (U.J.C.) the workers (C.T.C.), the women (F.M.C.), the small farmers (A.N.A.P.) and the neighbors in urban communities (C.D.R.). The puritan spirit is expressed by closing all bars and night clubs, and the abolition of cockfights and the state lottery.

The revolutionary leaders blame an exceptional drought for less agricultural output, state purchases, and consumer-goods supplies. But, though the weather has certainly been bad, other factors also had influence.

Many expropriated merchants used to buy part of the farm output at high prices, reducing the amount purchased by the state. A good portion acquired by the merchants was sold in the black market and bought by government opponents. Persons with money hired others to stand in the long queues. Thousands of counterrevolutionaries received food packages from abroad. Private merchants, and their employees, had incomes higher than those of state employees. In summary: the revolutionaries were worse paid and fed than the opponents of the government.

As the private-trade sector grew, the difficulties became aggravated into a vicious cycle: less state purchases, worse state supplies, expansion of rationings, increase of the blackmarket, and a widening gap in goods received between government supporters and opponents. The government hopes that the Offensive will put a halt to all this.

According to U.N. statistics, the growth of real G.N.P. (in constant prices) in 1962-66 was 1.9 percent per year. But, per capita, this meant a fall of 0.5 percent. (The Soviet average rate of growth of per capita G.N.P. in 1928-32 was 4.5 percent per year.) There was an annual decline of G.N.P. per capita of 4.4 percent in 1965-66. The situation had apparently not improved in 1968; the rough estimate shows a G.N.P. below that of 1966 and, in the meantime, the population has grown more than 4 percent.

Underlying reasons for the backward Cuban rate have been the decline in sugar and agricultural output, and the small proportion of G.N.P. devoted to investment until 1965. Causes of the latter have been the negative balance of trade, the increasing foreign debt, the large early outlay for social services such as education, health, social security and recreation, and the waste caused by disorganization, frequent changes in economic policy, inefficient investment, excessive bureaucracy, and redundant employment in state enterprises.

The percentage of gross national product that Cuba reinvests is low compared to what other socialist countries have done during parallel early periods of planning. Between 1961-66 Cuba reinvested an average of about 19 percent, compared to the U.S.S.R.'s 31 percent in 1928-37 and China's 25 percent in 1953-57. Castro estimates that to improve the economy 5 percent annually, 30 percent of G.N.P. must be reinvested each year. Cuba has not been capable of achieving that vital early goal of a socialist economy—huge capital accumulation. Further, since G.N.P. has declined, the only possibility for boosting investment is to drastically reduce consumption.

The revolutionary leaders are quite optimistic. According to official plans, 3,000 miles of roads will be built in 1968 and 24,000 miles by 1975. One hundred towns with 120 houses each are to be built within 10 years. By the end of 1970 the cement capacity is to be increased threefold. Cultivated land will increase by 65 percent in 1970-80, and Cuba will use half of all fertilizers programmed by South America for this period. The irrigation plans are grandiose: four million hectares in the next five years (total area of the country is 7.8 million hectares and in 1952 only 60,000 hectares were irrigated). To achieve this, various rivers (including the Cauto, the island's largest) will be diverted.

By 1970, 335,000 hectares of land are to be drained and planted with sugar cane, while another 300,000 will also be irrigated and planted. Thus by 1970 the goal of 10 million tons of sugar will be achieved. Total mechanization of sugar will be a reality in 1970-75. Windbreak curtains of trees will eliminate the threat that hurricanes and windstorms pose to sugar, coffee, tobacco, and bananas. Hundreds of thousands of citrus fruit and wood trees, and hundreds of millions of coffee trees, will be planted in more than 30,000 hectares of land that encircle the capital city ("Havana Greenbelt Project"). The annual average growth of agricultural output in 1970-80 is estimated at 13 percent. The expected success will assure enough consumer goods to end rationing. Economic abundance and better political education will make possible the new communist man.

What are the real chances of achieving these ambitious targets? It is too early to know, but a comparison with similar attempts by other socialist countries may throw some light. The Offensive notably resembles the Chinese "Great Leap Forward." Both campaigns emphasized the collectivization of small private enterprises, a huge labor mobilization, the endeavor to increase remarkably the rate of investment, spectacular plans to raise agricultural production (for example, the draining of the sea between the Isle of Pines and Cuba), a campaign to arouse revolutionary enthusiasm, and the elimination of the last remnants of economic incentives. Although large-scale repetition of the Chinese communal system has not taken place, such experiments have been under way since early 1967, the most conspicuous being the "San Andrés" commune in Pinar del Río province. Besides, the chances are that the remaining private farms should be collectivized soon.

There are other resemblances: the emphasis in ideology, the denunciation of foreign customs and influences (for example, boys' long hair, beards, and tight pants and girls' miniskirts have been banned in Cuba), the stress on revolutionary puritanism, and the exhortations to study the writings of the maximum leader.

But the "Great Leap Forward" was preceded by a series of favorable crops and economic successes. The opposite is true of Cuba; there the Offensive followed a series of failures in the sugar harvest (in 1963-64, 1966 and 1968). The results of radicalization could therefore be more severe and force a drastic shift, as happened in the U.S.S.R. in 1921 and in China in 1960.

Factors that brought the "Great Leap Forward" to failure are also latent in the Cuban Offensive. Reduction of material rewards and consumption and increase in exertion and sacrifice certainly have limits. If the state pressure goes beyond them, it could bring on open dissatisfaction. Castro reported open protests in early 1968, and he revealed late that year that 80 sabotages had taken place throughout the Island in six months. One-fourth caused millions of pesos in losses. Other public protests have been led by youngsters who destroyed state property and burned pictures of Che Guevara.

On the other hand, even if capital accumulation did result, it would not insure, by itself, rapid economic growth. Capital allocation for investment must be distributed and used with efficiency. State enterprises have used capital allotments without care about profit and loss, and this has resulted in financial irresponsibility. Andrés Vilariño, a Cuban economist, has said that investment inefficiency is one of the principal causes of declining productivity. According to Carlos Romeo, a Chilean economist working for the Cuban government, the nation has been unable to construct and get into operation the factories supplied by the socialist world (which were based on outdated technology to begin with) as fast as received. As a result, Dumont writes that "delicate machinery has piled up and sometimes rusted." Castro himself has added: "Today, machinery arrives, and because of ignorance, it is often put into the hands of persons who have not the slightest notion of what machinery is; of how to take care of it; of the type of maintenance, fuel or oil required for it. . . . A new machine that costs twenty or twenty-five thousand [dollars] in foreign exchange [therefore] becomes a piece of junk."

The Offensive programs are so vast that they would require an army of technicians and managers. But Cuba lacks these. Workers lacking expertise in agricultural chores and irrigation work may cause damage to crops and the water supply. Development of new crops without previous study may bring poor returns; for example, as much as one-third of the new coffee has been planted on mineral-deficient soil that will require expensive fertilization and irrigation.

Nationalizing private businesses has not overcome the inefficiency in state distribution and may make it worse because of inexperienced new managers. The now-banned black market did help production. Small farmers tried to raise their output in order to sell part of it at the high prices offered by merchants; and the merchants filled out state deficiencies in distribution. The small group of state employees with high salaries (technicians, managers, etc.) could buy in the black market goods absent from the state stores. In addition, the black market, small businesses, the reception of packages from abroad, and even bars were safety outlets for the uncommitted and the antagonistic. Less personal consumption eventually will lead to greater rationing. If this happens, more protests should be expected, as well as greater numbers wanting to leave the country, some of them with vital skills or expertise. It must be remembered that the Offensive is not a radical shift in economic policy but just an abrupt intensification. Hasty collectivization and eradication of individual initiative and material reward in 1962-67 created serious difficulties. The current radicalization may accentuate those problems.

Some isolated events provide some indication of what is happening. On March 1, 1968 (before the nationalization process began) the state procurement agency of Camagüey bought 126,000 kilograms of milk, but one month later (when the nationalization process was almost completed) such buyings fell by 2,000 kilograms. Ten days afterwards, a new decline of 10,000 kilograms was officially reported. The government alleges that this decline is due to a fall in production caused by the severe drought and announces a restriction in milk supply. The future will tell if drought was the only cause. Members of the A.N.A.P. can no longer sell their products at the high price paid by merchants. Farmers could find that to produce for the low prices offered by the state doesn't pay. Besides, these farmers possibly suspect that in the long run they will face the same fate as the merchants—so why take pains to keep up production?

Despite the high sugar target of nine million tons for 1969 (two million above the highest ever produced), Castro decreed sugar rationing at the beginning of this year to cut 200,000 tons from domestic consumption. This quantity will then be made available for foreign trade and investment. Although sugar consumption per capita is still high in Cuba (larger than in the United States), the main problem is that the people have been using sugar to fill in for foods in short supply.

The Prime Minister also announced that the rice crop in 1968 had been 50,000 tons. Rice production reached 323,000 metric tons in 1960 but steadily declined. Hence, the internal supply of this essential product of the Cuban diet was much worse in 1968 than in previous years.

Castro has forecast that 1969 would be a year of great work and hardship, "made up of 18 months." Most of the labor force would be cutting sugar cane in the fields continuously from November 1969, until July 1970, without the traditional recess for Christmas and New Year. Thus, 1969 has been christened the "Year of the Decisive Effort." Certainly no better name could have been chosen. In

1969-70 the entire viability of the economic policy of Castro's Cuba will be put to a crucial test. If the essential projects of the Offensive are successful, it is logical to expect a continuation and, perhaps, accentuation of the moral incentives. If, on the contrary, plans fail and political unrest increases, then we will see a return to more safe and tested practices both in ideology and economics.

April 1969

FURTHER READING SUGGESTED BY THE AUTHOR:

The Economic Transformation of Cuba by Edward Boorstein (New York: Monthly Review Press, 1968) is a descriptive study of the transformation of the Cuban economy in 1961-63.
Study on Cuba by Cuban Economic Research Project (Miami: The University of Miami Press, 1965), and *Cuba: Facts and Figures of an Economy in Ruins* by José M. Illan (Miami: Editorial AIP, 1964). These emphasize the pre-revolutionary situation and the early period of economic transformation.
"The Cuban Economy" in *Economic Survey for Latin America, 1963* (New York: ECLA, 1965) Part 4. This is the best economic analysis available for the period 1959-63, and includes abundant statistics.
Statistical Abstract Supplement: Cuba 1968 edited by Paul Roberts (Los Angeles: UCLA Latin American Center, scheduled for Spring 1969). This compilation of official Cuban statistics covers the prerevolutionary years, the years of transition, and the socialist years.
Cuba: The Economic and Social Revolution by Dudley Seers et al. (Chapel Hill: The University of North Carolina Press, 1964). This is a collection of essays based on field research done in 1962 and contains chapters on economic background, agriculture, industry, and education.

The Moral Economy
of a
Revolutionary Society

JOSEPH A. KAHL

Most commentaries on the Cuban revolution published in the United States stress its economic confusions and difficulties. We read about the "grey" atmosphere of Havana, in contrast to its prerevolutionary gaiety, and learn about long lines of customers waiting to buy, under the rationing system, the few articles to be seen in the stores.

A recent visit of a month in Cuba was enough to convince me of two points that do not deny the prevailing austerity but cast it in a new light:

First, the fundamental driving force behind the revolution and its first decade in power was not a plan for instant prosperity but rather a moral imperative to create a just and dignified society in contrast to memories of a degrading past. Thus the "gaiety" of Havana was dampened since much of it represented vice for tourists and decadent luxury for a handful of Cubans in the midst of a mass of impoverished fellow-citizens. Redistribution of wealth and the provision of jobs for the many unemployed were seen as the most important tasks; they have been accomplished.

Second, the Cuban economy has turned the corner and is about to produce new abundance. The first five years of emphasis on impractical industrialization have been succeeded by five years of intensive and rational investments in modern agriculture that are beginning to pay off. Only a person who sees the many new coffee and fruit trees in the Cordón, the greenbelt around Havana, planted by urban workers on weekends, or views the citrus trees on the Isle of Pines (renamed the Isle of Youth), planted by thousands of young people who volunteered for two years of work under pioneer conditions, or visits the cattle ranches in the province of Pinar del Río, which are upgrading the herds through advanced methods of artificial insemination, can appreciate the magnitude of new investment and its imminent productivity. When the new crops flow to market, the reconstruction of society will become clearer, since it will not be obscured by economic failures.

To understand the current scene, one must emphasize what is central to the Cubans themselves: The starting point was their society of the 1950's and the emotional revulsion against it that swept through the "generation of the Moncada," the young rebels who followed Fidel Castro in his ill-fated assault against the fortress of that name in 1953 and who stuck with him until they toppled Batista more than five years later. These were not men with a detailed economic blueprint for a new society; they were intensely nationalist Cubans who hated the corruption, the foreign influence, and the brutality of life around them. As Castro explained in his famous defense, "History Will Absolve Me," at the Moncada trial, the purpose of their revolt was to cleanse and purify the nation through heroic action.

Several times during my trip I heard groups reminiscing about the "bad old days." There seem to be a few standard stories that are elaborated with personal touches. The underlying theme is corruption. "Do you know that huge mansion of Senator X on Quinta Avenida?" (At first I thought this meant Fifth Avenue in New York, and then realized that it was a street in a luxurious Havana suburb, but the unintended double meaning conveys more truth than the literal denotation.) "Well, he got that through stealing money that was supposed to be used for schools in my province." Another person in the group would top the story by telling how rich an acquaintance of his became through the sale of admissions to public hospitals. "But what about that guy who controlled space in the Havana cemetery?" queried another.

One of the most popular programs on TV is a biweekly episode in the life of a senator (played by an actor who was a senator) who typifies the old political boss: A fat, cigar-smoking fellow who gulls peasants and workers with smooth talk ("let's all contribute for the new school"), and then runs off with the money to enjoy the "sinful" pleasures of Havana. This corruption is not seen as the result of the weakness of some men. It is interpreted as the inevitable consequence of capitalist society, particularly in underdeveloped countries. In such nations, where the mass of men are poor and uneducated, the few who are rich are uncontrolled in their appetites and powers. The final degrading touch in Cuba was the fact that elite position was based upon links to the United States, which directly or indirectly controlled so much of Cuban society. Foreigners or their local allies were seen as despoiling the body and soul of the nation.

One aging intellectual, an active revolutionary in the thirties and a more passive but approving one in the fifties, said, "Never forget that we lived for over a decade (if you count both of Batista's terms in office) under a particularly crude bunch, utterly lacking in education or refinement. They were sergeants who seized control and sold out to the American gangsters who ran the gambling and the prostitution. We had a lot to overcome."

One story told with relish concerns Batista's desire to become a member of the Yacht Club. Since he was a mulatto, he was not eligible. But with a $50,000 initiation fee, plus the construction at government expense of a series of canals that permitted many members to tie up their yachts at their back doors, he was permitted to join. Tourist guides love to point out the canals. They also indicate that the private beaches of the clubs are now open to the public, and the buildings are either schools or social centers for students.

To the corruption was added brutality. The men and women who made the revolution were young, often student leaders. During the struggle their ranks were decimated by tortures and cruelties. Indeed, thousands were killed in Batista's jails, far more than the few who died during guerrilla battles.

Although the fight against Batista was central, the Cubans date the beginning of their struggle for independence with the start of the revolt against Spain in 1868; they speak of "100 years of struggle" climaxed by the "triumph of the rebellion" against Batista, followed by "10 years of revolution," the latter referring to the efforts to build a new society. All of this was necessary in order to be free from Spain and from the United States. It gives them a deep identification with the people of Vietnam who are also fighting foreigners; the Cubans support the Communist forces, and view the war as a moral crusade. They see in it proof that American capitalism inevitably leads to imperialism, the exploitation of weaker nations, and the destruction of human decency.

When I talked with a group of young journalists-in-training at the offices of *Juventud Rebelde* (Rebellious Youth, daily newspaper of the Young Communist League), I confessed my skepticism of determinist theories of history.

I argued that Americans increasingly saw the Vietnam war as a tragic mistake and expressed the hope that we had learned a lesson from it. I appealed for a view of humanity that would rise above conflicts between capitalism and Communism, and criticized them for forcing every event into the mold of that conflict, thus turning their paper into a stereotype. With the tolerant, smug conviction of committed youth, tempered by Cuban politeness, they called me an "incurable romantic."

Schools all over the island remind children about Vietnam and its implications—indeed, many schools are named "Heroic Vietnam." One example conveys the entire lesson at once: Colored pencils, which are scarce, were passed out to school children. Then the teacher explained that they were even scarcer in Vietnam and asked the children voluntarily to return the pencils for shipment overseas. The teacher said every child gave back his pencil.

One of the key slogans on the big billboards surrounding the Plaza of the Revolution José Martí, where Fidel addressed about a million people last January 2, the tenth anniversary of the triumph of the rebellion, reads:

"El Camino Del Comunismo Es Crear Riqueza Con La Conciencia." Literally, it means "The Road of Communism Is to Create Wealth through *Conciencia.*" That last and key word conveys an amalgam of consciousness, conscience, conscientiousness, and commitment, and is perhaps the most repeated word in the Cuban language of revolution. The implication is that in the old society the mentality of the people was formed by money or the pursuit of money, and the motivation for work was the fear of poverty, but in the new society people will comprehend the need to work for the common good, and abundance will flow as a result of that understanding. Along with it will come a style of life that is cooperative and humane, and without "alienation," since work will be part of a voluntary social

experience.

Fidel bluntly expressed it on March 13, 1968:

We cannot encourage or even permit selfish attitudes among men if we don't want them to be guided by the instinct of selfishness, by the wolf, by the beast instinct. . . . The concept of socialism and communism, the concept of a higher society, implies a man devoid of those feelings; a man who has overcome such instinct at any cost, placing, above everything, his sense of solidarity and brotherhood among men. . . . If we are going to fail because we believe in man's ability, in his ability to improve, then we will fail; but we will never renounce our faith in mankind.

Society is to be reshaped in the pattern of comradeship of the guerrilla fighters of the Sierra Maestra. Some of the abstractions stem from Marx, but the Cuban color comes from the mountains. That is why Che Guevara, who continued to exemplify the values of the mountains even after the rebellion was won, is a martyr on the way to sanctification. And his phrase "the new man" is used to symbolize the core of revolutionary morality.

To the Cubans, the moral basis of the Revolution is fundamental, and its shifting economic plans are secondary, pragmatic experiments. The fact that per capita income may have gone down slightly is much less important to them than the fact that income is distributed more equally. Under Batista (and his predecessors) only a tiny fraction of the rural populace had the chance to eat meat, drink milk, wear shoes, visit a doctor, or send their children to school. *About a third were chronically unemployed. Now everyone has a job,* and the most important services are no longer scarce, or at least are evenly distributed.

Medical care is free, and for the first time it is spread throughout the island instead of being concentrated in Havana. Despite the exodus of many doctors to the United

States, enough have been trained to increase the total in practice up to 7,000. There are three medical schools instead of one, 32 teaching hospitals instead of four. The number of hospital beds has doubled to 40,000; more than 250 small clinics have been built in rural and urban neighborhoods; there are 48 rural general hospitals instead of only one. Vaccination and sanitary services have reached a level sufficient to eliminate malaria and polio—not a single case of either last year. The death rate has been reduced from 7.5 to 6.2 (the population is exceptionally young, which lowers the rate), and the life expectancy has risen to about 67 years. These are statistics appropriate to "developed" countries and are far ahead of the rest of Latin America. True, Cuba had a relatively good medical base before the revolution, but its extension to all parts of the country during a time of economic austerity is a considerable accomplishment.

There has been an even more marked expansion in education. The prerevolutionary rate of illiteracy was about 25 percent, and it has been reduced to 3 or 4 percent. Most children now stay in school through the sixth grade, or the end of primary education; the enrollments at that level have doubled to 1,444,000. (In the rest of Latin America, from 1960 through 1967, primary enrollment went up only 50 percent, and the proportion of children attending school increased from 48 to 56 percent. The absolute number of children *not* attending primary school increased, as a result of population growth, by some 2.5 million.) Cuban night-school classes at primary and secondary levels have almost half-a-million students. Adults are pressured into getting the sixth grade certificate, and then can continue if they wish. *Twenty-five percent of all Cubans, two of eight million, are registered in a classroom.*

Secondary-school enrollments almost tripled in the decade to 172,000. Vocational training at the secondary level has exploded. There were no schools of agronomy or fishing before; now almost 40,000 students study those subjects. Industrial schools have grown from 6,000 to 30,000 students, and university enrollments have doubled to 40,000. Students from rural areas without nearby schools receive scholarships to attend boarding schools or to go to the cities. About 250,000 students receive some form of scholarship aid; another 160,000 attend "semiboarding" schools that supply three meals a day.

A sharp redistribution of income was provided shortly after victory by a law which cut all rent in half; next year rent will be completely abolished. Meat is scarce, but all share the ration of three-quarters of a pound per week. Milk is rationed to children under seven and to the elderly, and school lunchrooms have milk in abundance; adults do without. In both city and countryside, I became aware of something strange to an observer who has travelled in many Latin American countries: *Not one person was without shoes.*

For the first time Cuba's Negroes—about one-third of the population—share equally in the goods and services and the civic respect of their society. They have been fully integrated in the schools and on the job. The sense of moral superiority about racial integration felt by Cuban leaders was brought home to me by a documentary film. (Short films are the one new art form that has flourished since the revolution; they are imaginative, avant-garde in style, usually didactic and political, but often humorous.) I saw it at a regular movie theatre along with a French cops-and-robbers film. It was entitled "Now," and featured the song of that name sung in English (with a very few subtitles in Spanish). Accompanying the song was a montage of still news photos of blacks in the United States being beaten by police, occasionally interspersed with quick views of the Lincoln Memorial or Martin Luther King; there was no commentary.

The new Cuban values are not against abundance. Quite

the contrary: Fidel promises that the decade of austerity
is over and the decade of plenty is beginning. He swears
that Cuba will jump from an underdeveloped to a developed society before the 1970's have ended. But he describes it as an abundance of discipline and restraint: Priorities will be set by reason and by plan, egoistic competition
that sets one man against another and degenerates into
selfishness and corruption will be absent, and men will
have learned to work hard and well because they understand the contribution they are making to the common
good—because they have *conciencia*. When all of this
comes about, differences in pay between engineers and
sweepers can be eliminated as unnecessary; indeed, money
itself will go.

These goals are being approached step-by-step. The first
problem was to overcome the idea that nirvana had ar-
rived the day after the triumph of the rebellion and everybody could loaf. As Fidel expressed it in his tenth-anni-
versary address:

The mirage of class society, of capitalist society, of
full store windows, created for the masses the illusory
idea that all that was necessary was to break the glass
and distribute the riches. But the mirage was based on
misery, on unemployment and underemployment. And
now the masses understand that riches must be created,
for they know how to add and subtract and multiply
and divide. When you divide among eight million people the production created by that type of society, even
the second-graders discover that it was a production of
misery. When 80 percent or 90 percent of the children
don't drink milk, 50,000 cows are enough, and there's
extra milk in the stores. But when you give milk to all
children born in this country, and every one without exception has this right, then 50,000 cows aren't enough,
nor 100,000, nor 200,000, but we need half-a-million.
Half-a-million milk cows are now growing in this coun-

try, and other half-millions will be born, and there will be a quart not only for the children but for all citizens of this country at a date not far distant.

At the beginning, our production did not grow—it decreased. And what we produced was in conditions of misery, sickness, hunger, evictions, dismissals. Cane was cut by hand, 15, 16, 17 hours a day. These bad conditions changed before we had the new machines, the new knowledge. From too much work, some substituted too little. Production went down to 3.8 million tons of sugar.

But now it has changed. In Latin America, agricultural production goes up 1, 2, or 3 percent a year—sometimes less than population growth. But in Cuba, production in 1970 will be double that in 1958. Something absolutely extraordinary, unprecedented. Actually, this doubling will come about in only the last 4 or 5 years. We are learning not only to add, but to multiply.

Thus Fidel proclaims that the first goal was to redistribute wealth and eliminate misery, the second to increase investment, and the third to provide abundance. The first is a fact, the second is well under way, and the third seems just around the bend, for the optimism not only in Havana but especially in the countryside where the work is being done begins to convince the visitor.

All admit that the industrialization drive of the first five years was a disaster—no raw materials, no engineers or skilled workers, no markets. But the new drive to technify and diversify agriculture appears to be on a sounder footing. Technicians are now graduating from the agronomy schools and returning from study abroad. Rice production tripled in 1968. Artificial insemination of cattle is proceeding rapidly, and increases in milk production from the new cross-bred herds are remarkable. New lands were cleared and irrigated, and the new sugar, citrus and coffee are growing. The socialist countries provide guaranteed markets for the sugar, meat and grapefruit—after all, Cuba is their only tropical partner. And all of Europe enjoys Havana cigars. This new output is not yet counted in the statistics of annual gross national product; but it is counted in the statistics of new acreage and new plantings and can be seen by the visitor who gets out of Havana. If the crops flow to market, then the coming decade will produce a deep shift in the Cuban scene.

Fidel promised a growth of agricultural output of 15 percent a year during the seventies. He said acreage will go up 65 percent (compared to 15 percent in Latin America); that Cuba will use one-half as much fertilizer as all the rest of Latin America combined. The main crops, in order of importance, will be sugar, cattle, citrus, tobacco, coffee. Citrus production went from about 100,000 tons in 1962 to over 150,000 tons now, and is scheduled to reach 4,500,-000 tons in 1980, close to current American production and double that of Israel. Sugar will go from a low of 3.8 million tons after the rebellion (a normal crop used to be between 5 and 6) to the goal for 1970 of 10 million tons, thereafter to be stabilized. New industries are being developed using agricultural raw materials. Even with a hefty discount for failures to reach the goals, the increases should be remarkable.

But what about the spirit of sacrifice, of dedication, of *conciencia?* Fidel claims that only in the past few years have the masses begun to understand. They have been led to this understanding partly by his own outstanding skill as a teacher. Listening to him in the Plaza or on the radio, I was surprised to find that most of his speaking was not political diatribe, the impression one gets from seeing his picture in our newspapers with his mouth open and his arm raised. Much of his talk is calmly didactic—patient explanation with colorful examples. He is a superb lecturer who can make the abstractions of economic development come alive. Incidentally, the speeches are now shorter than they were, down to about two hours.

Fidel's lectures are spread by militants, the Communist Party and the Young Communist League, who appear to number from 10 to 20 percent of most work groups. They are the soul of the revolution. The older ones, who are in their thirties or forties, fought in the mountains or in the underground. They are a proud bunch who conquered an army 10 times their number, and then stood off Goliath himself at Playa Girón (Bay of Pigs). They are convinced that willpower and heroism can accomplish anything. The younger militants have to be trained in the schools. As teenagers, many participated in the national mobilization that followed victory: the campaign to abolish illiteracy in 1961. Many city boys and girls lived with peasant families in isolated districts for several months and taught them to read and write, learning in return the hard facts of rural life.

Education is deeply politicized. Politics means much more than the study of Marxism-Leninism; above all, it means *conciencia* and hard work. A model student is one who masters his textbooks, volunteers for extra labor in the fields, and becomes a militant. The success of the attempt to produce abundance through commitment will depend upon the ability of these militants to maintain their enthusiasm after the initial crisis and challenge of establishing the new society has been outgrown, as well as their ability to transfer part of their enthusiasm to the masses.

I asked one Cuban friend, who himself had been a member of the student underground against Batista, how he expected his children to catch his enthusiasm for the new society, since they could not remember the old one and did not have heroic memories of participation in the rebellion. He responded: "It is a problem we are aware of. They learn from me and from the school. When I go out on Sunday to work in the Cordón, I try to take one of my two small children with me. They don't work, but they watch their father, and get the idea that such physical labor is honorable. They also see the fun we have, since I go with pals from the office and we kid around a lot. And in school they are taught about the goal of the revolution to create by cooperative work a society that is just and humane. And they learn to identify with the underprivileged around the world. They come to understand that our revolution cannot be complete until exploitation has ended everywhere—poor as we are, we send a few doctors or technicians to Algeria or Vietnam to help out."

Instead of the guerrilla bands of their fathers, these youngsters are taught to identify with work brigades, especially in the rural zones. I visited one boarding school in the provinces; it includes grades three through nine. Despite the fact that the pupils are the children of farmers, it is recognized that many will go on to advanced education. Yet rural and collective values are stressed, along with concentration on studies to the limit of individual abilities. For example, the children spend two hours a day in the fields surrounding the school, growing their own rice, fruit, and vegetables. And they do all the work of cleaning and service in the dormitories and the kitchens, except for a few professional male cooks and a few women who clean the bathrooms. Student tribunals, modeled after those in factories or collective farms, handle all problems of discipline.

The teachers, who are all under 21, share the collective life of the students; everybody stays on the grounds except for trips home every second weekend. The teachers convey subject matter and ideological commitment simultaneously. Most came from poor rural families and would have been denied an education under the old regime; they believe in the new one. Incidentally, they continue to study and improve themselves by taking correspondence courses; their distant tutor occasionally visits them and evaluates their work. Talking to them, one catches a spirit of constant effort at change and improvement, rather than "I've got my teaching certificate, now send me the salary check and let me follow the teacher's manual in peace."

Urban secondary schools and university departments as units work for a month or 45 days in the fields during the harvest period. Deans and professors and students live and work together. Rank is changed: the work boss gives the orders, and the professors comply along with the students. This program of "school to the country" not only supplies needed labor, but shapes the perceptions of the new generation. They understand from aching backs that farm labor is hard and is the base of the Cuban economy. They learn that the purpose of education in their country is to prepare technicians who will make such labor easier and more productive, not to supply soft careers to the educated man.

I think one unspoken lesson may be the most significant; they see their teachers, and their cabinet ministers, and Fidel himself working in the fields. The entire system takes on a legitimacy that is the opposite of the old corruption. Leadership means harder work than the average, and few special privileges. The pressures from such leadership may be resisted as being more than an ordinary citizen wishes to bear, for life is more than work; but those pressures will not be turned aside as false phrases coming from men whose purpose is personal enrichment through exploitation of others. Even the temporary visitor to the island begins to feel guilty if he does not volunteer to cut some cane.

The lessons of the schools are solidified on the job, where collective competition replaces individual competition. Several times a year, for each anniversary (that of Moncada on July 26, or the Triumph of the Rebellion on January 2, or May Day, etc.) awards are granted to top work units. One of the most coveted awards is "Héroes del Moncada," which grants the right to fly a flag announcing superiority. To get it (and keep it, since every year it must be won again), a garage, a restaurant, a hotel, a factory must meet or excel all work norms, must have a high number of "voluntary hours" of overtime labor, on the job or in the countryside, must show special desire to serve the public well, and must have everybody who lacks the 6th grade certificate in attendance at night school. Within the group, workers' committees have some leeway in deciding how much sick pay a man will get when he is ill, or exactly when his retirement will begin. The worker with *conciencia* gets an extra break.

Obviously, such a system does not "do away with material incentives" as the Cubans claim. What it does is tend to transfer identification of reward from the individual to the group. Everybody in the unit will share the honor of the flag; all of Cuba will have abundance, or nobody will. Even so, the individual gets direct rewards through some material advantages such as extended sick leave and by receiving prestige within the group, which must be particularly effective in motivating the young. *Conciencia* is not all giving; those who show it gain advantages.

For the moment, salary differences persist. The minimum old-age pension is now 60 pesos (equivalent at the official rate to 60 dollars) a month; the minimum wage appears to be about 85 pesos; cane-cutters will receive in 1969 a minimum of 96 pesos for a 24-day month; machine operators in the cane fields will earn from 110 to 160 pesos; the supposed maximum salary is 700 pesos. Until recently, workers were deliberately attracted to frontier zones by higher pay, but that policy has ended. The goal is to slowly eliminate pay differences as motivation evolves from *conciencia*. Overtime pay has just about been eliminated; minimums go up; and more and more types of consumption become free, thus reducing the importance of income. So far, education, medical care, sporting events, and burials; next year, rent.

In the meantime, strange remnants of the old society remain. For example, all owners of urban or rural real estate whose lands were confiscated receive two lifetime privileges: (1) they can live in their original houses without paying rent (one child of a small farmer can inherit the land) ; (2) they receive a pension in lieu of rental income, up to a maximum of 600 pesos a month. Thus hundreds, perhaps thousands, of former landlords are living on pensions in Havana and provide the main clientele for the fancy restaurants, since there is not much else to do with money—there are no cars, furs, jewels, or foreign tours to buy. The attitude of the new regime toward these people appears to be: In theory they were exploiters of the poor, but they are also unfortunate human beings who were brought up under a bad system and did not really understand what they were doing; so let them live and die in peace. And let them go to Miami if they insist.

The hardest, indeed, the impossible task for a tourist on a short visit is to penetrate the rhetoric of *conciencia* to find out how it really works. Try as one does to avoid it, the visitor ends up speaking mainly to leaders, to militants. With some previous contacts and some luck, he manages to have private conversations with a few people who are lukewarm, or even openly opposed to the system, but as he travels about the island he is attracted toward the new zones where the action is, and he is introduced to the local party chairman or the local school principal.

In private conversations, people are not afraid to talk; there is very little of the supreme caution and suspicion that I found in the Soviet Union in a visit in 1959 (the peak of Khrushchev's reform period). Cubans are not afraid of each other or to be seen with foreigners. So long as one avoids overt acts of hostility, such as attempting to flee the island without permission, or fomenting sabotage, one need not fear the police. Batista's cops were far more dangerous, and so from their own historical perspective, Cubans can deny that they live in a police state. Pressures come from the group, not from above, and they are constant and insidious, far more effective in shaping individual behavior than threats of official violence.

But how far does the ordinary citizen, the nonmilitant, go in granting his allegiance? Does he believe all the rhetoric or "tune it out" the way we do with TV commercials? When he "volunteers" for extra work, how free is the will, how generous the impulse? Only by living within a group over a period of time could one answer the question; the technique of participant observation would be the only way to find out.

There are some objective indicators, although they are not pure indexes of *conciencia*. Production declined after the triumph of the rebellion, but now seems to be restoring itself and on the verge of a major increase. Yet changes in motivation are only part of the reason. Turnover in the entire administrative system, the shift to and then away from industrialization, the flight of the old technicians and the training of new ones, the perfecting of group methods of behavior control—all of these also affect absenteeism and productivity.

Within youth itself, I suspect that the resistance to the rhetoric of the revolution is not so much counterrevolutionary as it is countersociety, a hunger for privacy, for a chance to develop individuality in an atmosphere of leisure. Every adolescent is not by nature a Spartan; some are Athenians, and they must suffer under the constant pressure to study, to work, and above all, to participate.

My own feeling is that the young militants are convinced they are building a superior society, and that they are probably carrying along the masses to a sufficient degree. To talk with them was profoundly moving, especially in contrast to the disillusion and cynicism of many of the best of young Americans. Cuban youths are not alienated, bitter, or "turned off." Some are a bit sad, since they often come from middle-class families and their own commitment to the revolution has separated them from their parents who fled the country. But most display a joy, a comradeship, a combination of a deep belief and an honest and playful sense of humor about it that is truly refreshing. They are dedicated but not pompous—an attractive generation, difficult to resist. After a while I worried less about the fact that I was spending too much time with leaders and not enough with followers, since I concluded that these leaders will shape the future.

Concerning internal affairs, the militants are not dogmatists. Indeed, they are proud of the fact that their Marxism-Leninism is pragmatic; they will try anything that might work. They admit that the early industrialization drive was a mistake. They say that anything they have done for ten years should be scrapped, since the essence of revolution is change. Fidel publicly begins to worry that maybe, at the age of 41, he is getting too old to be a revolutionary leader.

However, debates about internal policy are largely verbal: There are no channels for publishing openly critical arguments. The newspapers and magazines are monotonous reiterations of the official view. Occasionally a work of serious literature raises some doubts in a guarded vein. Last year two books were published that became test cases, a play by Anton Arrufat, *Siete Contra Tebas,* and a collection of poems by Heberto Padilla, *Fuera del Juego.* They received prizes from the international jury assembled each year by the Casa de las América, the Cuban institute for cultural interchange with Latin America. Then a committee of the Cuban National Union of Writers objected and said that the books contained "antirevolutionary concepts." The books were published with a prologue by the committee giving their criticisms; the authors were not molested and continue to work. Intellectuals are debating the implications of the incident and future policy.

When they look outside of their country, the Cuban view appears to become more dogmatic. Their knowledge of the world is a caricature of reality. True, those who wish may go to the National Library and read the London *Times* or *The New York Times* (I tried it—they are available, as they were not in the Soviet Union), but few bother. More listen to the Miami radio or watch the late show from Key West. Serious study of the outside world is nonexistent. The books and journals are scarce (because of foreign-exchange shortages, so they say, and thus the United States blockade), and besides, the major interest in the universities is technical competence plus motivation to build the new Cuba. The new generation of Cubans does not have much genuine curiousity about the outside; they are satisfied with the caricatures. Furthermore, they do not seem to care much about telling their own story to the United States. They know we receive a garbled picture of Cuba, but suspect we would not believe the truth.

This dogmatism is perhaps the automatic result of militant belief in the vision of utopia. True believers of any creed lose objectivity and curiosity. They know the answers in advance. American youthful militants (at least the white ones) have too often lost all belief and become nihilists and destroyers; Cuban youthful militants have the security of conviction and the narrowness that goes with it. They are building utopia, and it completely absorbs their energies. The independent intellectual, the critic of all societies and all beliefs, is a luxury they cannot afford.

The Cuban utopia has two colorations: One is Communist society; the other is *patria,* a Cuba free of foreign domination for the first time in its history. Every new threat from the United States reinforces patriotism and drives more people to support the regime. The economic and military aid from Russia is seen as help from a sympathetic and happily distant partner and not as a sign of control. The Cubans are Communists, but they are not Slavs and have no intention of becoming Russianized. They are something new and still not fully formed: Latin American

Communists.

Upon returning home, I read various articles by journalists who were in Cuba at the same time I was. It was striking to see how their observations reflected their perspectives. For example, the *Newsweek* correspondent who is head of the Paris bureau called Havana "the most depressing city on earth." My perspective comes from 15 years of study of various Latin American countries, but no previous experience in Cuba. I tended to notice the contrasts between the commitment of Cuban youth and the alienation of their counterparts in other Latin American countries. I was struck by the energy of a society moving under its own direction toward goals that emerged from its own history and needs. Surely nobody from Recife or Guatemala City would call Havana depressing.

Washington, of course, has its own perspective. It stresses that Cuba is dangerous because it is sending guerrilla fighters and arms to Latin American countries and thus stirring up trouble. Furthermore, Washington condemns these policies because they are based on violence. The Cubans dismiss this line and are convinced that it shows American duplicity. They point out that throughout Latin America military regimes keep themselves in power with United States guns and advice—they ask, why is American violence "good" and Cuban violence "bad"? Furthermore they indicate that the real threat from the United States is our system not our guns. They say we have dominated Latin America for a century, and yet ignorance, misery, corruption, and infant mortality go on year after year. They note that even United States critics now openly proclaim the failure of the Alliance for Progress. (Fidel quoted at length in his anniversary address from an article in the Spanish language edition of *Life* magazine, by a former State Department man.)

So far, Washington answers with more military aid for

internal supression, and new talk about increasing United States corporate investment—that is, compounding the disease. Yet the challenge from Cuba is not, I am sure, a few isolated guerrilleros; Che is dead, and it is more clear than ever that revolution cannot be exported.

The challenge from Cuba has not really begun. It will appear as a serious political threat when and if the Cuban economy begins to produce and the austerity fades away. Then the underlying moral thrust of the Cuban revolution can show itself, unstained by the economic difficulties that so far have distracted attention from the successes of social reconstruction. Young people in Latin America who are sick of stagnant societies and illegitimate leaders increasingly will be inspired by the vigorous example of Cuba. The militant dedication will seem to them an exhilerating life. They will try not to import it wholesale but to learn from it and to emulate it. Working for a subsidiary of General Motors or submitting to local generals in American uniforms will offer no satisfactory alternatives, for they contain no moral uplift. People who are demoralized seek a way out of despair, not a degrading handout in return for submission.

April 1969

FURTHER READING SUGGESTED BY THE AUTHOR:

Man and Society in Cuba, by Ernesto "Che" Guevara (Havana, 1965) is a statement of the theory of the "new man" to be nurtured by the new society. It is an important revision of Old Communist doctrine.

Castro's Cuba, Cuba's Fidel by Lee Lockwood (New York: Macmillan, 1967). Lockwood, a brilliant photographer, combines his pictures and a transcript of a five-day tape-recorded interview with Fidel Castro in 1965.

90 Miles From Home by Warren Miller (Boston: Little, Brown, 1961). A novelist describes his travels in Cuba in the early years of the revolution; he catches the spirit of the revolution in great detail.

Cuba-
Revolution Without
A Blueprint

MAURICE ZEITLIN

The world-historical significance of the Cuban revolution is that for the first time in the western hemisphere a revolution has been put through in the name of socialism. It is the first socialist revolution led by independent radicals throughout its most decisive phases. Even when they were to identify with the international Communist movement, and to fuse with the old Communists, they retained the clear initiative within the revolutionary leadership, and gained for Cuba a singular place among Communist states. The Cuban revolution has gone further, and has more profoundly and rapidly transformed the prerevolutionary social structure than has any other "socialist" revolution anywhere. Most of the fundamental transformation of the political economy—of property relations and of the class structure— occurred within a couple of years of the revolutionaries consolidation of power; and with the recent (March 1968) nationalization of some 55,000 small businesses, primarily in food retailing and services, virtually the entire economy is now in the public sector: In agriculture, 70 percent of the arable land is in the public sector, leaving only farms of less than 67 hectares (160 acres) to be worked by their owners.

What explains the rapidity and thoroughness of the Cuban revolution, compared not only to other national and social revolutions in our time, but to other "socialist" revolutions as well?—and, perhaps inseparable from this, why did it become a "socialist revolution," unlike, for instance, the social revolutions in Mexico and Bolivia?

The Cuban, Mexican, and Bolivian revolutions have certain similarities which are neither superficial nor unimportant. In each, there was a fundamental agrarian transformation that abolished the existing land tenure system and destroyed the economic base of the ruling strata in the countryside. In each, the old military apparatus was smashed and replaced with armed detachments (or militias) of peasants and workers. In each, strategic sectors of the national economy which were foreign-owned were nationalized. In Bolivia, the tin mines were occupied and run by the armed miners themselves. In Mexico, though late in the revolutionary process, the Cárdenas regime nationalized the oil industry.

These three revolutions, therefore, are unquestionably set apart from other so-called revolutions in Latin America. Nevertheless, the similarity between the Cuban revolution and the revolutions in Mexico and Bolivia is far less important than the major difference: Scarcely an aspect of the prerevolutionary social structure in Cuba has remained intact, primarily because of the expropriation of the former owning classes, the virtual elimination of private property in the system of production and distribution, and the establishment of a centrally-planned, publicly-owned economy.

What were the features of the prerevolutionary social structure in Cuba that determined the type of social structure created by the revolution? Somewhat differently: What were the constraints and the options that were given to the leaders of the Cuban revolution by the prerevolutionary social structure? What did they have to put up with, what was the social material they had to work with in order to make this revolution—in contrast, for instance, to those who led the revolutions and came to power in Russia, China, and Yugoslavia, or in Bolivia or Mexico? In the book which I wrote with Robert Scheer several years ago *(Cuba: Tragedy in Our Hemisphere)* we took the pre-revolutionary social structure as given and focused on the interaction between the United States and Cuba and in what way the interchange between them radicalized the revolution. Of course, the two are really inseparable, and it is likely that the interchange was itself determined by the prerevolutionary social structure. I want now to take that interchange as given, in order to search out the relevance of the prerevolutionary social structure itself.

My leading hypothesis is: Cuba's is the first socialist revolution to take place in a capitalist country—a country in which the owning class was capitalist and the direct producers were wage-workers. The argument may be stated in the following schematic working hypotheses:

Cuba's dominant economic class was capitalist—a peculiar type of capitalist class but a capitalist class nonetheless. There were no significant feudal or seignorial elements remaining in the upper economic strata. The major elements of the dominant strata were in exporting (mainly of sugar and other primary products) and its financing, importing (mainly luxury goods), and tourism, small-scale manufacture of consumer goods for the home market; and were agents, and representatives, investors in United States-owned manufacturing firms using equipment and materials imported from the United States. These elements tended to overlap and intertwine, and to be integrated by concrete economic interests and social and familial bonds. In short they formed the capitalist class. The agrarian component of this class was export-market oriented and employed wage-labor on a large scale in the sugar mills and cane fields. As a result, the revolution did not have to be anti-feudal.

Of the classes, the working class was the largest, the most cohesive, and the most politically conscious. It was an organized national class that spread throughout the country, and that had a durable revolutionary and socialist political culture set in motion by the anarcho-syndicalists and continued under the Communist leadership of the workers. This cannot be said of any other country in which revolutions in our time—whether anticolonial, nationalist, or Communist—have been put through. It cannot be said of prerevolutionary Russia certainly, where the Petrograd workers were an insignificant minority (in numbers) of the total population though decisive in the revolution. Nor certainly can it be said of prerevolutionary China, nor of Mexico, Bolivia, Algeria, nor of Vietnam. This may come as something of a conceptual shock, since the image of prerevolutionary Cuba held by many, whether friends or foes of the revolution, is that of a peasant society. Nor was it, in an important sense, an "underdeveloped" country. From the standpoint of an analysis of the economic system and class structure of prerevolutionary Cuba, I believe it is much more fruitful to view it as a relatively unevenly developed or misdeveloped capitalist country of a special colonial type.

In the agrarian sector, there was no subsistence peasantry, nor the nonwage tenant-labor characteristic of the *hacienda* or manorial economy. The vast majority of the economically active population employed in agriculture were wage workers. Improved working conditions and higher wages—working-class interests—rather than "land hunger" were their essential demands and aspirations, unlike the situation in other countries where revolutions calling themselves "socialist" have occurred. Moreover, what there was of a nonwage working population in Cuba's countryside was a small proprietor stratum—the *colonos*—who were integrated into the market economy and dependent on the large, economically strategic sugar "centrals" (production centers including mills, workers' housing and transportation) for credit, milling, and marketing; in the case of tobacco and coffee cultivation, there were also small proprietors and/or tenants whose overall economic significance was marginal. The agrarian sector was based on large-scale capitalist enterprises which employed both industrial and agricultural wage workers.

What strengthened the hand of the ruling class in other social revolutions in this century was a mass social base, largely in the countryside, which they could mobilize as allies to defend their own interests. A counterrevolutionary movement in these countries was possible because the rulers still had legitimacy in and social control of the rural population. It was no historical accident that a bloody civil war was required in revolutionary Russia to put down the counterrevolution, that three decades of armed warfare preceded the triumph of the Chinese Communists, or that the Mexican revolutionaries had to violently confront and overcome the combined might of the Catholic Church and *hacendados*—the large landowners. The Cuban revolutionaries (and this is not to detract from their own extraordinary abilities) did not have to confront a similar situation. The landed upper stratum had been virtually expropriated by the development of capitalism much before the revolution.

Of course, Cuban capitalism was absentee-owned, foreign-controlled, and quasi-colonial. This meant that not only did the ruling strata not have roots in the countryside but that, indeed, they had no significant independent base of economic power in the country as a whole. The so-called Cuban capitalist class was dependent on American capitalism—politically, militarily, economically. Because of this dependency, they also lacked social legitimacy. The justification of their rule stood nakedly revealed as their control of the means of violence. They stayed in power because they had a military regime (and behind it the power of the United States government) to protect them, not because anyone believed that they *deserved* power or that they had the *right* to rule. They were illegitimate in the eyes of virtually the entire population because they had shown their incapacity to rule effectively.

Contrast this for a moment with the situation of the ruling strata in Chile, since it is the only other country in the western hemisphere in which a mass-based Marxian socialist movement has had relative durability—and is rooted predominantly in the working class. Despite this, Chile's ruling strata have considerable legitimacy. A coalition of owning strata which is both landed and industrial has been able to demonstrate its capacity to rule over a period of a century without either foreign control or the intervention of the military as an autonomous social force. In the countryside, the *hacendados* ruled a peasantry involved in tenant-labor, living on the great *fundos* and exploited through seignorial and paternalistic relations. Only recently has agrarian agitation and organization begun to shake this stability. This is in contrast to the instability and massive struggles that characterized the Cuban past, and in which the struggles were directed against a class that was scarcely considered (and perhaps scarcely considered itself) Cuban.

This contrast in the capacity of these classes to rule is also shown by the fact that Chilean political stability and parliamentary democracy have been inseparable. In Cuba, the forms of political democracy associated with capitalism had, so to speak, exhausted themselves. The brief interregnum of political democracy was considered to be a sham and not substantially more relevant to the needs of Cuba as a nation and to the interests of its people than military rule. Parties and politicians associated with Cuba's "Congress" were all but universally held in contempt. Parliamentary democracy as the legitimate mode of representative government and the bounds within which major conflicts ought to be resolved and government policy determined had lost legitimacy, if indeed it ever existed; a major ideological obstacle to revolutionary change had, therefore, been eroded well before the revolutionaries took power.

Eroded also had been whatever ideological dominion over the great majority of workers and "peasants" the Catholic Church may once have possessed. The Cuban upper strata, therefore, lacked the advantage of a significant ally that ruling classes confronted by revolutionary movements have usually had—an ally whose means of social control and moral suasion supported the existing social order and clothed revolutionary movements in the guise of mammon. That is not to say that the Church hierarchy did not oppose the social revolution. But because the communicants of the Church were drawn largely from the upper and upper-middle urban strata, and little from the countryside or peasantry, its weight in the struggle was not decisive. (It was neither a large land owner nor did it have church centers, schools, monasteries or nunneries scattered throughout the country—these scarcely existed.) Moreover, it was one of the peculiar benefits (or consequences) of direct United States occupation in the founding years of the Republic that Church and State were separated, and the American presence was a secularizing and rationalizing influence.

Large-scale enterprise in the countryside and the intermingling of industrial and agricultural workers in the sugar centrals permeated the country largely with capitalist, rationalistic, secular, antitraditional values and norms of conduct. In this sense, the country was *prepared* for development—the only thing lacking being the revolution itself which took control over the economy and the means of violence from capitalists, both foreign and domestic, and put it in the hands of a sovereign Cuban state.

Whereas the ruling strata lacked legitimacy and had no independent ideology that was expressive of their own peculiar interests and that they could impose on society at large, there was in the working class of Cuba a socialist political culture (of anarcho-syndicalist and Communist elements) born in an insurrectionary past, which had already existed for no less than three decades (and far longer in segments such as the tobacco workers). The outlook of the typical worker toward the system was impregnated by socialist ideas; what is most important, the vision of a future without capitalism was most firmly and widely held by the most decisive sectors of the working class. This is what Max Weber would have called a "simple historical fact" of such significance that without taking it into account one cannot understand the socialist revolution. If it was not the vision of the majority of workers in town and country, the dominant vision among them was, nonetheless anticapitalist, antiimperialist, and socialist. Even the essentially reformist and middle-class leadership of the Auténtico (and later *Ortodoxo*) party which had considerable influence among workers since the aborted revolution of the 1930s, and which was the only opposition of consequence to the Communists in the working class, also clothed its actions and program in a quasi-socialist rhetoric. Its influence among workers, however, was not of the same order as Communist influence and was debilitated by the widespread corruption of the Autentico leadership. Most working-class struggles, whatever the leadership and however narrow the economic demands, tended to take on the political slogans of antiimperialism and anticapitalism; it was their one consistent theme. The immediate ends of the struggle and the broader political aims—however tenuously—were linked. Thus, the historically significant impact on the workers' consciousness.

The *Report on Cuba* of the International Bank for

Reconstruction and Development concluded that in the years of the most clandestine activity of the Communists about one-fourth of all workers (in 1950) "were secretly sympathetic to them"; I found, when I interviewed a national sample of workers in 1962, that some 29 percent claimed to have been partisans of the Communists before the revolution. Most important, the ideas held by workers who were non-Communist, even anti-Communist, also tended to be suffused by socialist content. As the *Report* also pointed out, "nearly all the popular education of working people on how an economic system works and what might be done to improve it came first from the anarcho-syndicalists, and most recently—and most effectively—from the Communists." It was, I believe, as naturally a part of the Cuban workers' conceptions of the system, their interests, and of the creation of a world which abolished their exploitation, as bread-and-butter unionism is "natural" to workers in the United States. Both resulted from given historical conditions in which the role of leadership (durable and institutional) was crucial. From the standpoint of the development of the socialist revolution, the importance of this simple historic fact cannot be exaggerated. Despite the vacillations, zigzags, and opportunism of the Communists, one thing occurred: the infusion in the workers of a vision that transcended the Communist leadership itself. The workers could in fact, abandon the Communists for Fidel to seek the fulfillment of the vision the Communists once represented. When the Revolutionary Government was established, it had a mass working-class base that likely was beyond its leaders in its vision of the society to be created by the revolution. This is in striking contrast to the situation in other countries in which the revolutionary leaders were far beyond their own mass base. The fact of a socialist political culture in the working class —a nationally-based, cohesive working class—combined with the force of nationalism and antiimperialism, created a potent revolutionary force waiting to be tapped by the revolutionary leaders once they took power.

Cuba, moreover, was in certain important respects a developed country. I say in important respects and emphasize at the same time the very uneven development of the country. Advanced industrial technology and primitive agricultural implements coexisted in interdependence within the same system. On the one hand, as James O'Connor has shown, economic institutions generally appearing in wealthy capitalist countries were fundamental in Cuba's prerevolutionary market structure. Production and distribution tended to be controlled by a few firms and producer's associations, and output, wages, prices, and earnings were determined within the framework of such market controls. Thus, Cuba had a vast reservoir of untapped, under-utilized and misutilized resources which the revolutionary government could utilize by reordering and planning the objectives of production and distribution. A relatively developed infrastructure, obviously colonial in nature and possessing its attendant problems but nonetheless of great significance, already was established in Cuba before the revolution. Both in terms of its ability to communicate with the nation as a whole and to provide it with immediate, visible, and concrete benefits from the revolution, the revolutionaries enjoyed great advantages compared to the leaders of other social revolutions in our time. The revolutionary government could do what other revolutions' leaders could not do: They could put through an immediate and significant redistribution of the national income and improve the conditions of the masses within, so to speak, the first days of taking power. The share of the national income received by wage workers was increased by roughly one-third, according to conservative estimates (such as those by Felipe Pozos, former President of the National Bank of Cuba, in exile). This provided a cement between the regime and the masses in the early phases of the revolution which other revolutionary governments could not create in this way.

The sugar-central, wage-labor, agrarian complex also made it possible to create relatively rapidly and easily a socialist agrarian sector—virtually by shifting the locus of control within it and reorganizing and reordering the objectives of production. This, again, is very much in contrast to the prerevolutionary agrarian structure inherited by other revolutionaries. Most important, the labor movement in the countryside already included wage laborers within the central labor organization; industrial and agricultural workers associated naturally in the countryside and created bonds of social solidarity. Thus, the classical revolutionary slogan of the alliance and unity of workers and peasants was already, in a very important sense, a durable social fact before the revolutionaries came to power. The factories in the field, the sugar centrals containing the sugar mills and associated lands, provided a situation in which agricultural workers living and working on the central's lands came into more or less regular contact with industrial workers. Also, the agricultural worker himself, or his brother, or friends, may have worked at one time as a cane-cutter and another in the sugar mills, providing the industrial and agricultural worker with a fund of common experiences and perceptions. Poor proprietors also often worked in similar situations.

These centrals were, in addition, not only centers of industrial production and a basis for the creation of natural social bonds between "peasants" and workers, but also centers of political agitation and education. The most important prerevolutionary political base of the Communists was here. Forty-one percent of the sugar-central workers, compared to 30 percent of urban workers who had those occupations before the revolution, said in our interviews with them in 1962 that they were prerevolutionary supporters of the Communists. Therefore, for all these reasons, the very same acts which the Revolutionary Government would have to take from the standpoint of economic rationality, that is, to spur development, were also acts that helped secure its mass social and political base.

Think for a moment of what confronted the Soviet Communists—what, from their standpoint, they found necessary to do to destroy the old agrarian structure and replace it with a modern one. The New Economic Plan, distribution of the land and then its forcible expropriation from the very same peasants upon whom the regime rested—none of this was necessary in Cuba (nor the vast chaos and destruction of civil war). On the contrary, almost the very act of taking over and nationalizing the sugar centrals cemented the already extant bonds between workers and peasants; their working conditions and living conditions were immediately and positively transformed. The immediate and long-range interests of both were identical; each needed the other in past struggles and each was affected similarly by the fluctuations in the economy. With the revolution, these common interests became even more intimately associated. Contrast this with the Mexican revolution, where the "red battalions" of Carranza's workers helped to put down peasant rebellion, or with peasants and tin miners played off against each other in Bolivia in order to maintain the *status quo*. Contrast this with the massive repression of the peasantry under Stalin, and it indicates the profound importance of the prerevolutionary social structure in determining the pace and direction of the revolution in Cuba.

The Cuban revolutionaries—whatever their extraordinary abilities, especially Fidel's—came to power in a society whose prerevolutionary social structure endowed them with vast advantages compared to the leaders of other major social revolutions in this century. Neither the capacity of the revolutionary leaders nor their actions and reaction to the United States (nor the presence of the Soviet Union as a potential ally) can be separated from the *reality* (the "real world") of the revolutionary process. However, I think that it can be shown also that the rapidity and thoroughness (as well as the humane and libertarian aspects which I have not discussed here) of the Cuban revolution, and its movement into socialism, to a great extent were the result of the prerevolutionary social structure. Once a leadership came to power in Cuba that was really committed to a national solution to her problems—once revolutionaries committed to economic development and an independent national existence took power, and would brook no interference (indeed, a highly problematic "if" provided by Fidel, Che, and their comrades), the revolution's course was profoundly influenced by the prerevolutionary social structure. Therefore, Fidel led a socialist revolution almost without knowing it and the Communists were virtually dragged into socialism by the *fidelistas* because history made this possible.

This is essentially the text of a paper prepared for a lecture series under the auspices of the Center for Latin American Studies of the University of California at Berkeley, on the "Caribbean in Crisis" in the spring of 1968. It is published here with the Center's permission. The paper was also delivered at the Annual Meeting of the American Historical Association this past December, at a Joint Session with the Conference on Latin American History.

April 1969

FURTHER READING SUGGESTED BY THE AUTHOR:

The Origins of Socialism in Cuba by James O'Connor (Ithaca, N.Y.: Cornell University Press, to be published September, 1969).

Fidel Castro by Herbert Matthews (New York: Simon and Schuster, to be published in May).

Cuba: The Making of a Revolution by Ramón Eduardo Ruiz (Amherst, Mass.: University of Massachusetts Press, 1968).

United States·Cuba Relations: Beyond the Quarantine

IRVING LOUIS HOROWITZ

In what must be ranked as one of its more curious, if not downright bizarre, "intelligence reports" on Latin America, the widely distributed *Parade* magazine (Feb. 16, 1969) stated in its lead item: "Ten years ago Cuba was a corrupt, exciting, competitive, ambitious island with extremes of poverty and wealth. Havana was filled with 40,000 prostitutes, pimps, vendors of 'feelthy postcards.' Bars and nightclubs thrived. The U.S. Mafia partnered with Batista cronies ran the gambling apparatus. American tourists by the thousands flocked to the casinos. Money could buy everything, and there was everything to buy. Today, a decade after the Fidel Castro takeover and government by Communist edict, Havana is a sad, shabby, hopeless city of nothingness. There is no freedom to travel, dissent, start a business, buy property, assemble, talk, print, write, educate one's children."

This remarkable statement illustrates the political schizophrenia which engulfs the Jet Set attitudes of some Americans toward Cuba. The Puritan Spirit would prefer that Havana return to the status of a "Sin City" as a prelude to reevaluation of the Cuban regime. We expect freedom to

131

be defined as moral license in Havana but not in Boston. The official posture of the United States had been that diplomatic recognition of Cuba must be preceded by a Cuban cleansing. This in turn is defined by Robert Mc-Closky, Undersecretary of State, as an end to the "export" of revolution in the hemisphere (without any corresponding closure to the export of reaction from the hemisphere), and now apparently, Cuban willingness to reimport the gamblers, vendors, and fleshpots. The time for simple truths is now: Diplomatic recognition is not equivalent to a papal blessing, only to an appreciation that there are sufficiently important grounds for business and government interests to have direct intercourse with what is after all a neighboring nation.

The arguments used by the United States in denying the need for diplomatic recognition to China simply do not hold with respect to Cuba (leaving aside whether the arguments are even meaningful with respect to China). First, Cuba is a geographically proximate neighbor. Second, the flow of refugees in both directions is large enough to warrant some direct legal ties. Third, Cuba has in fact not "exported" its revolution, and whether it is even trying to do so is a far from settled point. Fourth, the need to regularize air traffic between the two countries has become urgent enough for both nations to warrant reestablishment of regular air runs without threats of intimidation or security checks.

The Department of State has a peculiarly moralistic way of interpreting de jure recognition. Underlying this withholding of recognition is not simply a legal disclaimer for what United States citizens may do in Cuba—this is but a passport dodge; it is the notion that Cuba can be starved into submission by the economic boycotts that the absence of diplomatic exchanges entails. The simple psychological fact that people under external pressure may react by greater effort, by greater sacrifice, apparently does not penetrate the

Latin American desks in the State Department. Indeed, I sometimes think that the "magic" in Cuba's heroic economy, what Joseph A. Kahl describes as the system of *conciencia,* has at least as much to do with United States blindness as with Fidel Castro's well-established charisma.

The need of the moment is some universally recognized principles of American foreign policy, or at least precepts that can be accepted throughout Latin America. Our government has no trouble recognizing or working with right-wing governments, which are presumably also out of favor, such as Paraguay and Haiti. And it will even grin and bear it when a military regime such as that of Peru engages in expropriations. Thus, if United States foreign policy is inconsistent with respect to established norms of diplomatic behavior, it is thoroughly consistent with a tradition of cold-war animosity for any left-wing ground swell in Latin America. The Monroe Doctrine stands between the United States and Cuba. The simple recognition of the Bolívar Doctrine of Latin American solidarity is the only answer that Cuba can effectively give. That the age of "doctrines" represents the leftover baggage of the 19th century will either be recognized by all concerned, or, as the late President John F. Kennedy said, "the whole thing's going to be won or lost, right here in Latin America."

What would be the payoffs in reestablishing diplomatic relations between the United States and Cuba? For the United States the advantages are, first, the uniform treatment of hemispheric neighbors, irrespective of political systems—and hence, an expectation of less suspicion of our motives; second, the possibility that the present artificial dependencies of Cuba upon the Soviet Union can be considerably eased; third, a nonmilitary solution to a hostile relation with a power "only 90 miles from home," and a possibility of easing the continuing crisis of Guantanamo Base. For Cuba, the advantages would be a reduced military budget with the assurance of a nonaggressive big-power neighbor; second, an easing of the travel and commercial restrictions which now seriously cripple the Cuban recovery effort; and finally, a lessening of dependence on the socialist bloc for raw materials and foodstuffs which could be obtained more easily and for less from North America. Cuba must begin to recognize that its fierce policy of independence has created the sorts of tensions with China and the Soviet Union that can better be managed by expanding and not contracting diplomatic options. It serves little purpose for Castro to denounce the normalization of relationships between eastern European countries and other Latin American states. More effective would be Cuba's own move to normalize and, hence, lessen world tensions by more serious moves toward diplomatic exchanges.

The prospects for diplomatic exchanges, while dim, do exist. The geographic proximity of the two nations must itself be reckoned as a factor. But more, the new openness of both the Cuban and United States governments toward nongovernmental-level exchanges, particularly from scholars interested in the hemisphere's problems, and from professional men having mutual concerns that have no bearing on the cold war, are good omens. But against these factors are arrayed the studied hostility of Robert McClosky to any change in status between the two powers; and beyond this, the absence of any conditioning of the American population to live in a world where Communist regimes are perceived as legitimate. This raises the touchiest and perhaps most decisive objection to diplomatic exchange: the existence of several hundred thousand Cuban exiles living in mainland United States.

This clustering of Cuban exiles, primarily in several large eastern seaboard cities from Miami to New York, serves as a powerful lobby against normalization of Cuban-U.S. relations. While for Castro their absence from Cuba lessened an internal threat to his regime, their presence in the United States makes settlement well-nigh impossible without shouts of betrayal. The Cuban exile communities have in effect reconstituted themselves as a "little Cuba," recreating the privileged structure and professional hierarchy that existed in prerevolutionary Cuba. This mini-world now exists as a pressure group to deny the present in the name of the past. It could well be that attempts to re-establish relations would unleash a series of invasion attempts that could only compromise the United States. Moreover, an attempted "two Cubas" policy, like the "two Chinas" policy, would prove entirely dysfunctional. Instead of promoting a genuine wedge between pro-Communist and anti-Communist forces, it would place the United States in the absurd position of dealing de jure with what is de facto impotent or nonexistent; and conversely, dealing de facto with regimes that are not recognized as legal entities.

It would be foolish to assert that acts of governmental rationality would resolve all problems, or that the bitterness and hostilities that exist are irrational or chimerical. The act of diplomacy may have to be made in the face of the egotistical petulance of the Cuban regime. This would not mean that the United States need renounce its objections to the Cuban Communist regime and how it has unfolded —even though these objections often include serious distortions of the record. Nor is it required that Cuba celebrate the United States (and hence possibly jeopardize its position with the Soviet Union). Neither is it necessary nor creditable for *fidelistas* to reply to the United States with exaggerated defenses of Cuban activities and apologies for "aberrations" in the revolutionary course. Higher apologetics, made as they are in the name of historical absolution, nevertheless cannot disguise the degree to which current Cuban realities are a far cry from early promises.

Over the years during which the Cuban revolution hardened, I pointed out that both in institutional and structural terms Cuba was transformed from a participatory democracy into a mass dictatorship. The public good has become a bludgeon employed against the private self. In this sense, one might say that Fidel represents the most articulate and certainly the boldest leader in the "socialist camp," but at the most, he can be credited with being a genteel Stalinist. The cult of personality continues unabated. The absence of criticism from within is notorious. The role of the Communist Party remains supreme.

Since the completion of my own evaluation of the stages of the Cuban regime, first undertaken in *New Politics* (1965), and extended to cover the Tricontinental phase, in *Trans*-action (1967), little has happened to alter the judgments therein made. And sadly, the brutal invasion of Czechoslovakia by Soviet troops was defended by Castro in sycophantic terms.

We are told by Castro in his statement of August 23, 1968, that "Czechoslovakia was moving toward a counter-revolutionary situation, toward capitalism and into the arms of imperialism. It was absolutely necessary, at all costs, in one way or another, to prevent this eventuality from taking place." It is not that Fidel is infatuated with the Warsaw Pact nations. Quite the contrary. He is quite aware of their hypocritical cant. Yet reasons of State prevail in his thinking. This underscores the simple fact that Castro is a Cuban nationalist first, and a Latin revolutionist second. Nothing that has happened since the pleasant declarations of international solidarity of the Tricontinental has changed this.

What is particularly disturbing is the political pathology behind the exaggerated declarations against Czechoslovakia. The "evidence" Castro provides that the Czechs were turning capitalist was wrapped up in the opinion that "anything that begins to receive the praise, support or enthusiastic applause of the imperialist press naturally should arouse suspicions." God help Fidel if the United States imperialist press decides to shower its affections on him. Presumably this would be evidence for an invasion of Cuba by Warsaw Pact nations to defend the poor Cubans from capitalism. And as if the decision to support Soviet occupation were not difficult enough on the face of it, there was the followup report in *Granma,* the official organ of the Cuban Communist Party, telling the world of the "unanimous support for Fidel's statements on Czechoslovakia"— all of this just "a few hours after" the Castro speech. We are assured that this unanimous support was at a "grassroots level," from such "independent" groups as the Committee for the Defense of the Revolution, the Young Communist League, and the Central Organization of Cuban Trade Unions.

Castro's agony is that he cannot act on his basic instinct that the cornerstone of the present antiimperialist struggle is between large powers and small nations. His assaults on *every other small nation* singled out for attack by the Soviet Union makes his dilemma acute. This is made unmistakably clear in Cuba's stepped-up assaults on the Yugoslav Communist Party—with a ferocity rivaling only that of the Albanians. The charge of capitalist restorationism and that Tito is the "lapdog of imperialism" makes no effort at honest analysis of what the Yugoslavian regime is about, or what it has meant to the people of that country to have resisted the yoke of economic inferiority and political impotence since 1948—a good decade before there even was a Cuban socialism.

Finally, there has been the condemnation of Israeli "aggression," and joint statements fatuously issued in collaboration with Algeria, condemning Israel as a "tool of imperialism." Again, not the slightest effort at sophistication or education of the Cuban people into the realities of middle-eastern feudalism. Not the slightest effort at making plain the *prima facie* similarities that exist between Israel and Cuba.

These things cannot go unnoticed. Nor can the absurd situation in which one man speaks for the nation, and thus relieves all others of the political responsibility for saying what is true or the moral responsibility for doing what is right. It is Fidel on medicine; Fidel on the sugar harvest of 1969; Fidel on genetics; Fidel opening a polyclinic; Fidel on dam construction. And always in strident terms: "Before the Revolution ceases to be, not one counterrevolutionary will remain with his head on his shoulders." In this same speech on "The Committee for the Defense of the Revolution" (Sept. 29, 1968), we are also told: ". . . no liberalism whatsoever! No softening whatsoever. A revolutionary people, a strong people—this is what is needed throughout these years." And always this same man interprets what is liberalism, what is revolutionism.

There is a price for development under any political system. But what the Cuban leadership has been unwilling to face is the converse equation, namely, the price for a political system to achieve development. If there is no other way to rapid economic and social development in Latin America than the Cuban model, at least let us face uncomfortable facts squarely. Let us have the courage to ask frankly what the price of development is, and state the feasible political conditions for allowing the people to decide whether they are willing to pay such a price. To provide scientific characterization is not "destructive criticism," but a basic obligation imposed by the nature of social analysis. We must continue to provide characterizations, because they are the stuff of which social science is made. And if ideologists of the right are displeased, and apologists of the left outraged—so be it. The same situation is true in nearly every area touched by vital human interests and passions. To lift the pink slip of a society is to see things that are not necessarily pretty. That there are those "scholars" who would deny the right of social investigators to give a hard look is only a trifle less disconcerting than those "politicos" who reject the right of criticism about the regimes in the world. Such expediency is misanthropic, a vicious blurring of alternatives to the dismal way things are.

More than a decade has elapsed since the victory of the July 26 Movement led by Fidel Castro and Ernesto Che Guevara. In that period, revolutionary euphoria, along with counterrevolutionary passions, have had a chance to simmer down. Cuba, for its part, has had to confront the tasks of governing a nation; while counterrevolutionary factions now know how costly "civic action" is, both in human and material terms. This is as it should be. For in nation-building as in child-rearing, mistakes of the past often do not so much get rectified as they get bypassed in the gradual recognition that problems of self-governance and international power are both harder and more complex than the going rhetoric would have it.

Adjustment to the limits of empire is no easy matter for the United States. Yet it can and must be made. Europe has made the adjustment to third-world nationalisms, and now it is our turn to do likewise. As Brazilian Archbishop Helder Camara pointed out, the United States must adjust to the "realities of revolution." There must be a termination of "continental excommunication" of Cuba, based as it is on "sterile hate." The belief of the Archbishop that Cuba should be reintegrated into the Latin American community "with due respect for her political option and acceptance of her autonomy as a sovereign nation" is clearly the cornerstone of any future relationships. Hopefully, it will not take another decennial celebration of the Cuban regime to bring about the historically obvious and the politically necessary.

Since this is an age for designing scenarios with the potentiality of reducing conflict, one might establish certain stages by means of which a reestablishment of normal relations between Cuba and the United States might occur.

■ *First:* Given the joint interest of both parties in reducing and eliminating the "hijacking" of aircraft to Havana, members of the Civil Aeronautics Boards of each nation might get together and discuss ways of arriving at such an end. Discussions would also cover an end to the alleged photographing and fingerprinting by the F.B.I. and the C.I.A. of every person who makes the Mexico-Havana run. This could then be followed, still at the same level of exchange, by a conference on establishing regular passenger service between New York, Miami (and other cities in the United States), and Havana. Included in this discussion would be the sale and upgrading of Cuban aircraft that would increase the safety factor and also help make Cuban Airlines more viable as an international carrier.

■ *Second:* This could be followed by a commercial conference that would discuss lifting the informal and formal United States ban on shipping commodities and raw materials to Cuba, and at the same time, would examine the problem of indemnification to United States corporations of property, machinery, and factories expropriated in the 1959-1961 period. Although the Castro government postponed any such settlement indefinitely, it never denied an ultimate responsibility for such indemnification.

■ *Third:* This level of exchange would probably be the most difficult, since it would involve military and political figures long implicated in the present impasse between the two governments. Yet, a conference might be structured so that a successful outcome was at least possible. The conference would essentially involve conditions for a tradeoff between the United States presence in Guantanamo Bay and the complete dismantling and removal of Cuban SAM [surface-to-air-missile] weapons. A strong case could be made that both the United States Naval Base and the Soviet missile emplacements are obsolete and thoroughly useless, even if a military engagement between the two nations were to occur. As evidence, one could cite the Playa Girón (Bay of Pigs) experience where neither a naval presence or a missile apparatus was of any value.

■ *Fourth:* If the third stage could be satisfactorily concluded, this would pave the way for a conference of the Organization of American States. At this diplomatic level, the entire Inter-American Defense Treaty apparatus could be reviewed. Clearly the risks at this point would be highest for the United States, since its entire faith in right-wing military regimes would itself come under review. However, given the evidence that such regimes behave capriciously and against the best interests of the United States (such as in the Peruvian and Brazilian takeovers by the hard-line military juntas), it might well be that the Department of State would be receptive to a restructuring of the Inter-American system along lines that would include Cuba as an essential member. Cuba does have a military establishment, and that military establishment has a direct interest in the tasks of hemispheric security, at least as it affects Cuba's security. Even at the time Cuba was expelled from the Organization of American States, there was bitter opposition to this move by the big powers: Chile, Mexico, Uruguay, and Costa Rica, among others, voiced strong dissent against the ostracism of Cuba. Any move to reestablish hemispheric contacts would be met with wide favor throughout Latin America.

■ *Fifth:* At this point, talks leading to the full resumption of diplomatic relations might be undertaken. These talks might be held either jointly or separately with special meetings of the OAS. They could take up questions of the status of Cuban refugees, the free exchange of everything from currency to scholars, and even arrange for cultural and scientific conferences with a high scientific input-output—such as conferences of agricultural and engineering specialists—and a low ideological input.

To those who might argue that United States "imperialism" or Cuban "Stalinism" are incompatible with such progressive reconciliation, one can only cite the evidence of history. Relatively cordial relationships were worked out between the United States and the Soviet Union in the

1930's and 1940's. Indeed, the behavior of both nations in their foreign policies was prudent precisely to the degree that there was internal regimentation. Foreign policy is historically an area not especially subject to popular or mass checks, and there is little reason to assume that the situation would be or need be different with respect to United States-Cuban relations. In other words, I am not suggesting that an ideological change of heart is necessary, or even that such stages of a concordat would result in the internal liberalization of either of the two antagonists. The point is that given the relative autonomy of foreign policy in both countries one might well expect a genuine easing of hemispheric tensions.

Surely, problems will remain. No attempt is being made to compromise the integrity of the two regimes involved— or the worth of capitalism and socialism as such. However, if United States and Cuban relations are to be different in the future, some such program of staged cooperation will become necessary. In the meantime, in advance of even the first stage of negotiations, each side can contribute to a lessening of tensions by a change of slogans, if not of heart. The Cubans might consider the following: *Verdad en lugar de patria; sobreviviremos en lugar de venceremos; vida en lugar de muerte.* [Truth in place of patriotism; we will survive in place of we will win; life in place of death.] And the United States might follow suit with a similar new set of formulas to live by: *Diplomacy in place of duplicity; fairness in place of fanaticism; self-determination in place of grand design.* In this wide-open world of human will all things are possible, even peace between neighboring countries.

April 1969

FURTHER READING SUGGESTED BY THE AUTHOR:

Books and monographs about the Cuban situation which are worthwhile from a social science viewpoint are scarce; but useful literature relating to Cuban-American relations is downright rare. Under the circumstances it is best to read the various "position" volumes and simply make the proper intellectual adjustments.

A History of Cuba and Its Relations with the United States by Phillip Foner (New York: International Publishers, 1963). This orthodox Communist presentation combines a rich historical overview with pedestrian Marxism.

Cuba and the United States: Long Range Perspectives edited by John Plank (Washington, D.C.: The Brookings Institution, 1967) is a useful compendium, which attempts to fashion a liberal, yet official-sounding, United States response toward "the troubled island."

The Cuban Invasion: Chronicle of a Disaster by Karl E. Meyer and Tad Szulc (New York: Praeger, 1962) is a tough journalistic appraisal of American adventurism and its political fallout for the hemisphere.

Cuba: Tragedy in Our Hemisphere by Maurice Zeitlin and Robert Scheer (New York: Grove Press, 1963) contains material on the relationships between the United States and Cuba from the Platt Amendment to the Bay of Pigs adventure. Prorevolutionary regime, but intelligently so.

The best single source for Cuban attitudes toward the United States is contained in the publication *Granma,* which is the official organ of the Central Committee of the Communist Party. It appears weekly.

The Editor

Irving Louis Horowitz is Chairman of the Department of Sociology of Livingston College at Rutgers University, Director of Studies in Comparative International Development there, and Editor-in-Chief of *trans*action magazine. He has worked extensively in the area of Latin American affairs and social policy, and has held teaching and research posts at the University of Buenos Aires and the National University of Mexico.

Among his books in the area are *Professing Sociology: Studies in the Life Cycle of Social Science; Latin American Radicalism: A Documentary Report of Left and Nationalist Movements* (with Josue de Castro and John Gerassi); *The Rise and Fall of Project Camelot: Studies in the Relationship between Social Science and Practical Politics; Three Worlds of Development: The Theory and Practice of International Stratification; The War Game; Revolution in Brazil: Politics and Society in a Development Nation;* and the forthcoming *Masses in Latin America.*

His current interests are in linking a systematic theory of political sociology to the concrete experiences of Third World nations, particularly those in Latin America with which he has had long past contact.